UNCOMMON *Beauty*

UNCOMMON *Beauty*

Tyndale House Publishers, Inc.
Carol Stream, Illinois

7 qualities of a
      beautiful woman

CYNTHIA HEALD

Library of Congress Cataloging-in-Publication Data

Heald, Cynthia.
   Uncommon beauty : 7 qualities of a beautiful woman / Cynthia Heald.
     p. cm.
   Includes bibliographical references and index.
   ISBN-13: 978-1-4143-0085-6 (sc)
   ISBN-10: 1-4143-0085-9 (sc)
1. Christian women—Religious life. 2. Self-actualization (Psychology) in women.
3. Self-actualization (Psychology)—Religious aspects—Christianity. I. Title.
   BV4527.H3987 2007
   248.8'43—dc22   2007002533

Printed in the United States of America

13 12 11 10 09 08 07
7 6 5 4 3 2 1

I *lovingly dedicate this book on inner beauty
to the lovely young women in our family:*

My daughters, Melinda and Shelly, and
My daughters-in-law, Cathy and Brenna.

How blessed I am that each of you is uncommonly beautiful.

❧ Contents

A Certain Something

You can take no credit for beauty at sixteen. But if you are beautiful at sixty, it will be your soul's own doing.[1]

MARIE STOOPS

In a delightful scene in my favorite novel, *Pride and Prejudice,* the characters discuss the attributes of an "accomplished" woman. Miss Bingley observes, "A woman must have a thorough knowledge of music, singing, drawing, dancing, and the modern languages, to deserve the word; and besides all this, she must possess a certain something in her air and manner of walking, the tone of her voice, her address and expressions, or the word will be but half deserved."[2]

While Miss Bingley was rarely insightful, in this

instance I agree with her statement. To be considered truly accomplished—talented, cultured, elegant, or competent—a woman must have "a certain something" in her air: an air of dignity or an air of security in who she is as a person. She is set apart as special, not only by what she has achieved, but also by her conduct or bearing. She has an indefinable quality, "a certain something," that enhances her accomplishments.

The same can be said of the attributes of a "beautiful" woman. For just as Jane Austen reminds us that performance alone does not necessarily make us accomplished, I think that physical beauty alone does not necessarily make us beautiful.

Growing up, I remember hearing the old adage "Beauty is as beauty does." What I understood from that saying is that although someone might be attractive physically, how that person lived really determined whether or not she was beautiful. Often a woman's actions and reactions can easily negate any outward beauty she might have.

Just as a woman's lack of inner character can mar her good looks, a beautiful soul can render a plain face lovely. Ruth Graham's Chinese nanny is a good example. Wang Nai Nai was depicted as "a homely old soul." Ruth describes this plain-featured woman: "Her nose was unusually broad and flat, and there was a mole on the side of it. Her eyes were little slits with short eyelashes, framed by laugh wrinkles. Her mouth was wide and kind. A peasant's face. A pleasant peasant's face. Mother was right. She was a homely old soul. But what did that matter; she was loving. I would have sworn her beautiful."[3]

The truth of Ruth's perceptions is reflected in Shakespeare's writings: "O! How much more doth beauty beauteous seem, by that sweet ornament which truth doth give!"[4] Indeed true beauty is recognized by authenticity and sincerity of character.

A French proverb also echoes that thought: "Beauty, unaccompanied by virtue, is a flower without perfume."[5] Beauty that blesses is beauty that leaves a sweet fragrance. Decades later Ruth Bell Graham remembered Wang Nai Nai with tenderness: "We children loved her. Everyone did."[6]

Beauty that blesses is beauty that leaves a sweet fragrance.

Probably since the beginning of time, outward beauty has been extolled and prized. Even the Bible

tells us that "People judge by outward appearance."[7]
Our culture is no different.

I remember my high school yearbook had a special
section titled, "You'd know our school by its beauties."
Over one hundred photographs were sent to Joe Paster-
nak, a Hollywood motion picture producer, and he
had the assignment of choosing the nine most beautiful
girls for the year. These nine photos were probably the
most popular section of our yearbook, more so than the
pictures of the different classes, sports teams, and various clubs and activities. Beauty was clearly valued and
defined by physical attributes alone.

Today we publicize and honor the "100 Most
Beautiful." Every facet of the beauty industry advertises
and entices women to become as beautiful as possible.
If we do not consider ourselves attractive, then we have
the options of cosmetic surgery, makeovers, diets, and
beauty treatments of every description.

We have even become a society accustomed to "air-
brushed" beauty. I smiled at the story of Elizabeth the
Queen Mother, who was selecting a photograph from a
recent sitting. Cecil Beaton, the photographer, suggested
that he could have the picture discreetly retouched to
conceal a few wrinkles. The Queen Mother rejected his

suggestion. "I would not want it to be thought that I had lived for all these years without having anything to show for it," she explained.[8] Her response is refreshing in light of our seeming obsession with looking young at all costs.

We need to pay attention to our outward appearance, but not to the extent that it overshadows our concern for inner beauty. Herbert Spencer remarked, "The saying that beauty is but skin deep is but a skin-deep saying."[9] Inner beauty bestows on us that "certain something" that sets us apart, gives our life meaning, and graces us with beauty even when we are sixty.

> *Inner beauty bestows on us that "certain something" that sets us apart, gives our life meaning, and graces us with beauty even when we are sixty.*

It is this inner loveliness that I have chosen to call *uncommon beauty.* It is uncommon because it is rare and not readily discerned. It can be sensed and observed only in a woman's conduct or bearing. It is a refreshing "air" that attracts and causes others to look past our physical attributes and appreciate who we really are inside.

Perhaps it is time again to examine several "sweet ornaments of truth" that will encourage women to pursue and cultivate that elusive beauty or special *air* that can spring only from our character—the "beauty beauteous."

When I think about a woman whom I admire and consider to be beautiful, I tend to think first of her inner qualities—whether she is gracious, considerate of others, courageous, wise. Beauty, to me, is seen in a woman whose face mirrors her acceptance of who she is, her contentment with where she is, and her enthusiasm for people and life.

Beauty, to me, is seen in a woman whose face mirrors her acceptance of who she is, her contentment with where she is, and her enthusiasm for people and life.

Because I value inner beauty, I have chosen to examine seven qualities that I think make a woman beautiful: passion, wisdom, integrity, selflessness, graciousness, contentment, and courage. I chose seven because the number represents wholeness and

completeness. The traits I chose came from my own
reflections as well as conversations with women and men
in response to my question, "What comes to your mind
when you hear the phrase *a beautiful woman*?" Certainly
other qualities could be considered, but after careful
contemplation I felt that these seven characteristics are
at least a good foundation for a discussion about inner
beauty.

To make these seven qualities come to life, I have
chosen key women from history, literature, the Bible,
and our society to illustrate each of these attributes.
It was a painstaking process to choose representative
women for each section, for if I have learned nothing else, I have discovered the incredible impact that
so many "beautiful" women have made on our world.
I also realized that most of the women I chose exemplified several if not all of the qualities. It seems that each
attribute tends to strengthen and encourage the growth
of the other qualities.

I tried to narrow most of my choices to what I
would call "ordinary" women—women with whom
I could readily identify. I avoided choosing women
who were unusually gifted in music, art, or literature.
I wanted women who could be easily emulated, for

my desire is that the lives of these women will inspire anyone, no matter how young or old, to say, "I want to develop these qualities in my life. I want to be in the process of becoming a woman of uncommon beauty."

Although the women we will discuss were ordinary, they became beautiful by choosing to live extraordinarily. They were comfortable with who they were, they rose above their circumstances, and they persevered. Their lives have encouraged me to take risks, to seek wisdom, and to live selflessly. It is so easy for me to get caught up in my own world and to seek comfort for myself alone. It is easy for me to focus more on my outward appearance than to develop gracious character. But as I have studied the lives of these women, I have learned that lasting beauty is bestowed on those who possess qualities that impart "a certain something," qualities that are the "soul's own doing," which can only be described as uncommonly beautiful.

> *Though we travel the world over to find the beautiful,*
> *we must carry it with us or we find it not.*[10]
>
> RALPH WALDO EMERSON

Questions for Reflection and Discussion

1. Complete this sentence: A beautiful woman is someone who . . .

2. When you think about beauty, what qualities come to mind?

3. What are your thoughts about the emphasis our society places on physical beauty?

4. What stereotypes does our culture give us of beauty?

5. To what extent do you think we should be concerned about our physical attributes?

6. In your experience, who models or has modeled uncommon beauty for you?

7. Are you comfortable with your physical appearance?
    Why or why not?

8. How do others view your inner qualities?

9. In what ways would you like to become an
    uncommonly beautiful woman?*

*To facilitate group discussion and personal study, see pages 171-74 for
Scripture verses related to each chapter in the book.

CHAPTER 1 *Passion*

*Far away, there in the sunshine,
are my highest aspirations. I may
not reach them, but I can look up
and see their beauty, believe in
them, and try to follow them.*[1]

LOUISA MAY ALCOTT

Linda was not what you would call pretty, but she was attractive because of the warmth and energy I sensed as I talked with her. I met her several years ago at a conference and was immediately captivated by her spirit of adventure and zest for life.

As a young adult, Linda determined that each year she would explore a new challenge. She wanted to expand her horizons, to experience life to its fullest. She hiked popular trails, took a variety of courses at a nearby college, learned to fly-fish, traveled to prominent historical and recreational sites, and learned a new language. The year I met her, she had signed up to skydive. As I left her, I thought, *She has uncommon beauty.*

It was refreshing to meet someone who was adventurous and eager to grow. As I reflected on Linda's life, I realized it was *passion* that propelled her beyond her comfort zone to experience the world around her. She was not willing to let life settle into a tedious routine. I think Linda's desire to embrace life is what drew me to her and is what made her beautiful in my eyes.

I resonate with Linda's passion. I, too, want to make the most of the life I have. If it's possible to have a new experience or to learn something interesting, then I want to do it. I don't want life to pass me by. I don't want to come to the end of my life and have regrets for not living as fully as I could have lived.

A few years ago my husband, Jack, and I hiked the thirty-three-mile Milford Track through the wild fjord country of New Zealand. The challenging trail is considered to be one of the finest walks in the world. Although the three-day hike was strenuous, the majestic scenery was well worth our effort. The cascading water-falls, glacially carved valleys, alpine flowers, and native birds left us with treasured memories. Jack and I are so glad we made the trip—before we were too old to walk!

The word *passion* is commonly equated with ardent romance, but this strong, energetic word can be used to describe the intense feelings and convictions we

---
Main Entry: pas·sion
Pronunciation: 'pa-shən
a: emotion **b:** ardent affection **c:** an intense desire, feeling, or conviction **d:** fervor **e:** zeal **f:** ardor **g:** enthusiasm

---

have about life. When I think of a woman who has passion, I think about her zest for living, her sense of purpose, and her desire to grow. A passionate woman radiates a confident "aliveness," an underlying excite-ment for life.

A woman who is passionate knows why she gets up in the morning. She is motivated to experience life as fully as she can and to remain hopeful in the midst of a busy and discordant world. Her passion propels her to reach for her highest aspirations, and it is this desire that produces a sparkle of inner beauty—the "beauty beauteous," as Shakespeare wrote.

I have an acquaintance who differs from Linda in every way. This woman is physically very attractive. Her hair shines, her clothes are stylish, but she lacks passion. When I am around her, she seems to be apathetic and bored with life. For various reasons this woman has chosen to create her own little world within herself. She expects life to come to her. She is not proactive but is complacent and complaining. She projects an "air" of indifference and pessimism. Her physical beauty pales in the presence of her joyless and purposeless spirit. Because her heart is without passion, her world is small.

> The world stands out on either side
> No wider than the heart is wide;
> Above the world is stretched the sky,
> No higher than the soul is high.[2]
>
> EDNA ST. VINCENT MILLAY

Passion to Explore

I vividly remember the January morning in 1986 when the space shuttle *Challenger* exploded just seventy-three seconds after blastoff. I had just dropped off my parents at the airport, turned on the radio, and heard the stunning, tragic news. Along with the rest of the nation, I was more aware and interested in this shuttle launch because of Christa McAuliffe, the first civilian and

teacher to fly aboard a shuttle. I was intrigued with this
adventuresome and engaging young woman. Because I
had also been a teacher, her passion for learning and
her willingness to widen her world captured my heart.

In 1984, when the National Aeronautics and Space
Administration wanted to revive interest in the space
program, they considered allowing an ordinary citizen
to be trained as an astronaut. They wanted a person who
could communicate enthusiasm and the significance
of space travel. President Reagan decided it should be
"one of America's finest, a teacher."

Christa's friends encouraged her to apply to the
Teacher in Space program. After completing an elev-
en-page application, she became one of 11,500 appli-
cants. She was surprised when she was chosen because
many of the people who applied were accomplished
scholars. She considered herself to be just an aver-
age woman. And in a way she was. This mother of two
children was a typical suburban woman who taught in
high school, played tennis, and volunteered at the local
hospital.

But Christa had "a certain something" that set
her apart from others. The students of Concord High
School in Concord, New Hampshire, flocked to her

social studies classes in order to learn from this enthusiastic, passionate teacher. They considered her an "inspirational human being, a marvelous teacher who made their lessons come alive."[3] Because Christa believed in providing hands-on learning experiences, she was known as the "The Field Trip Teacher."

Christa was eager to go on the shuttle mission. When she was interviewed, she said, "I think just opening up the door, having this ordinary person fly, says a lot for the future." Christa began training in the fall of 1985, and after 114 hours of instruction she was ready to take, in her own words, the "Ultimate Field Trip."

Christa McAuliffe personified passion: a zest for life, a desire to grow, a confident aliveness. Her mother, Grace Corrigan, wrote, "Christa lived. She never just sat back and existed. Christa always accomplished everything that she was capable of accomplishing. She extended her own limitations. She cared about her fellow human beings. She did the ordinary, but she did it well and unfailingly."[4]

Passion is doing the ordinary well and unfailingly.

What an ideal definition of passion: doing the
ordinary well and unfailingly. These words perfectly
describe Christa. Her zeal for making her life count
reinforced her legacy of doing the ordinary thought-
fully and faithfully. Like Edna St. Vincent Millay,
Christa knew that her world could be no wider than
her heart and that she could experience life only as fully
as her soul would allow. Although Christa lived to be
only thirty-seven years old, she will be remembered as
a passionate young woman who far away there, in the
sunshine, reached for her highest aspirations.

> *You don't get to choose how you're going to die. Or when. You can
> decide how you're going to live now.*[5]
>
> JOAN BAEZ

Passion for What Is Right

One woman who decided how she was going to live was
Mary Harris "Mother" Jones. Around the turn of the
twentieth century this widow and seamstress unrelenting-
ly worked to better conditions for the common laborer,
particularly miners. She was called the "miner's angel"
because she tirelessly fought for shorter hours, better
pay, and the right of workers to unionize. "She was a true

folk heroine, the 'Jeanne d'Arc of the miners.'" Mary "was a benevolent fanatic, a Celtic blend of sentiment and fire, of sweetness and fight." She believed that "the militant, not the meek, shall inherit the earth."[6] Mother Jones was passionate!

Another woman with a passion for what is right was Ida Bell Wells-Barnett. Ida was born into slavery six months before the signing of the Emancipation Proclamation. She was an ardent and outspoken advocate for black civil and economic rights as well as women's rights. "Her fiery and fearless one-woman crusade to end the infamous practice of lynching makes her especially worthy of recognition. . . . Her courage and lifelong commitment to racial justice have made her one of the most preeminent black leaders of all time."[7] Certainly Ida left the world better and more beautiful because of her passion for human rights.

Another woman whose passion had an impact on issues of human rights was Dorothea Lange, a photojournalist hired by the War Relocation Authority during World War II to take pictures of the Japanese-Americans sent to internment camps after the bombing of Pearl Harbor. Dorothea used her passion for photography to capture not only the stark realities of the armed camps but also the raw courage of the detainees. Her photos were so real that the government—her employer—censored many of them. After her death, her photographs were exhibited in the Whitney Museum. When A. D. Coleman, a *New York Times* art critic, visited the exhibit, he wrote, "Lange's photographs . . . convey the feeling of the victims as well as the facts of the crime." Dorothea's passion helped people see the truth.

These passionate women not only helped others to see the truth but also *lived* the truth. Passion is like that. When we are deeply passionate, we take on the world and take no thought about ourselves. We willingly strive and even sacrifice for what is good and right, and in the process we become uncommonly beautiful.

> *When we are deeply passionate,*
> *we willingly strive and even sacrifice*
> *for what is good and right.*

What if you believed something passionately but knew that if you followed your belief, you would be defying authority and could die as a result? What would you do? Would you have the courage to follow your conscience?

Antigone, the main character in Sophocles' ancient play *Antigone,* was caught in a moral dilemma. Both of her brothers had died, but the king decreed that only one of the brothers could receive a proper and honorable burial. Antigone could not bear the thought that her other brother, whom the king perceived to be a traitor, would not be buried. His body would be left to decay, exposed to the animals and sun. To complicate matters, the king ordered that anyone who buried this man would be put to death.

What was Antigone to do? Compelled by her belief that moral law is higher than human law, she chose to violate the king's command and bury her brother, knowing she might die as a result.

When confronted with unfairness and a violation of rights, Antigone nobly chose to value what was right over what was decreed. Her passion compelled her to commit what she called a "crime of devotion."

Although Antigone ultimately took her own life, she had no second thoughts. These are among her last words:

> No, I *do not suffer from the fact of death,*
> But *if* I *had let my own brother stay unburied*
> I *would have suffered all the pain* I *do not feel now.*[8]

Antigone's sacrifice may seem extreme and unmerited in today's world, but her burning desire, her passion to remain true to her conscience rather than conform to society, challenges me to live truly and boldly in my world.

It is interesting that during World War II, a version of *Antigone* was rewritten and used to strengthen and encourage the resistance against the Nazis. Her courage, her fervency to stand for what is right, emboldened the spirits of those who were fighting injustice.

> People *living deeply have no fear of death.*[9]
>
> ANAIS NIN

Passion for People

Just as the Japanese-Americans whom Dorothea Lange photographed were forced to leave their homes because of their racial and ethnic heritage, Priscilla was forced out of her home because she was a Jew. In AD 50, the Roman emperor expelled all Jews from

Rome, creating chaos in the lives of Priscilla and her husband, Aquila.[10]

Feeling the sting of persecution, she packed her belongings and left everything she knew—her home, her friends, and her familiar surroundings—to find refuge in a foreign country. After a thousand-mile journey, she and her husband settled in Corinth, a Greek city known for its wealth, luxury, and immorality. They knew very few people in the city and were forced to start over.

Instead of bemoaning her fate, Priscilla turned to the things she was passionate about: her faith and her love for people. She opened her heart and her home to people who needed friendship and encouragement.

Priscilla and Aquila were successful tentmakers by trade, and they immediately set up shop in their house. They met another tentmaker, a Jew named Paul, who was unmarried and needed the comfort of a home. He experienced Priscilla's warm hospitality when he lived and worked with them for a period of time. I can only imagine the number of people who knocked on her door—those coming to have tents made or mended, and those who came to visit with the great teacher, the apostle Paul.

After traveling with Paul to the city of Ephesus,

Priscilla and her husband established a church that met in their home. They later returned to Corinth and eventually to Rome, where in both places they welcomed into their home a congregation of believers. Persecution was still a real threat, and the couple faced great risk as they ministered to many people. I believe that it was Priscilla's passion for life that enabled her to graciously labor alongside her husband, to entertain, and to encourage many people in their faith.

Paul mentioned in his letter to the Roman church that Priscilla and Aquila had risked their lives for him. It is not clear what Paul was referring to, but it has been suggested that perhaps during the Ephesian riots, Priscilla and her husband had saved Paul from harm or death. A loving wife, a humble tentmaker, an ardent follower of Christ, Priscilla personified passion throughout her life.

Each in her own way, Christa, Antigone, and Priscilla rose to the occasion and reached for their highest aspirations. Each was defined by passion. Each illustrated the truth that a woman does not have to be known as a beauty to be considered beautiful. Passion adorns when it is deeply embedded in the heart and arises freely to grace its bearer.

We never know how high we are
Till we are called to rise;
And then, if we are true to plan,
Our statures touch the skies.[11]

EMILY DICKINSON

Passion out of Balance

The women whose stories we've examined are remembered with affection because their passion consisted of a courageous fervency that enriched their lives and the lives of others. Their passion did not *dominate* their lives, but it permeated and guided their everyday decisions. Their zest for life—kept in balance—produced an uncommon beauty.

Sometimes the beauty of passion is its subtlety. An overly passionate woman is often too eager, too forceful, and extreme in her beliefs. I am not especially drawn to excessive personalities who tend to focus exclusively on their wants and special interests.

Barbara became just such a person after she volunteered with a certain charity. Her admirable desire to help soon dominated her life, and she lost all sense of perspective. She neglected her family. She ignored her friends and turned every conversation into a commercial for her cause. Her extreme drivenness did not beautify; it actually made her unattractive.

Another woman whose passion was out of balance was Queen Jezebel. Driven by her self-centeredness, this queen used her passion to get whatever she wanted. She had an innocent man killed because he would not sell some land her husband wanted. She was so intimidating that the prophet Elijah ran for his life because the queen had sworn to have him killed within twenty-four hours. In writing about women in the Bible, Herbert Lockyer said of Jezebel, "A gifted woman, she prostituted all her gifts for the furtherance of evil, and her misdirected talents became a curse."[12] Jezebel's passion was tragically out of control, and it produced a woman who is remembered with contempt.

Becoming a Passionate Woman

How can we become passionate women? How can we acquire or develop a poised, passionate spirit? Unfortunately, we can't just decide, "I will now be a passionate woman." But we can examine our lives by asking a few questions: What do I get excited about? Why do I get up in the morning? What social concerns or causes stir my

passion? In what aspects of my life do I want to grow?
What have I always wanted to do?

As we answer these questions, we can begin to
awaken a passionate spirit. Passion is choosing to do
what you really are enthusiastic about. And sometimes
the fulfillment of your passion may take a lifetime. My
friend Suzanne has taken almost twenty years to get a
graduate degree in archaeology. As time allowed, in
the midst of raising her children, she studied, took
classes, and pursued her passion. At age seventy-five
Marie, a widow, enrolled in a ballroom dance class,
thus fulfilling a lifelong desire. Linda determined
to pursue one new interest a year—a skill, a craft, a
language, a trip. She was flexible so that her choices
were determined by the circumstances of her life at
the time.

> *Passion is choosing to do what you
> really are enthusiastic about.*

Passion is realizing you don't want just to exist;
you want to be engaged in life in some way. When I
was a young woman, I wanted to become accomplished
in some field, possibly literature or history. So, newly

married and recently graduated from college with a
degree in English, I convinced my veterinarian husband
to accompany me to a Great Books course at the local
library. This was the beginning of my lifelong enthusiasm for reading and studying. My passion to read is
most accommodating, for I have been able to read in
the midst of raising four children, helping my husband
deliver puppies, traveling, and being involved in various
activities.

You can nurture a passionate spirit by deciding to
embrace your life and to live as fully as you can. Listen
to Sara's philosophy about life: "'I pursue what scares
me. I always ask myself, "If you were afraid, would you
do it?" And if the answer is yes, I take a breath and
go for it.' Such thinking led Sara to pursue stand-up
comedy when she was afraid of public speaking and
climb the side of a hot air balloon at 10,000 feet when
she was scared of heights."[13]

Passion is knowing what your purpose is and
being true to what you know is right. It is allowing an
inner fire to ignite your spirit and warm your soul
and all others that you touch. After Christa McAuliffe
married, she continued her education by earning
a master's degree. She taught law, economics, and

American history to her students. She also developed a course entitled "The American Woman." She had no idea at the time that she would become an American woman who would be remembered and honored for decades.

> *Passion is knowing what your purpose is and being true to what you know is right.*

Each of the women we have read about in this chapter reached for her highest aspirations, and in her own unique way her stature "touched the skies." Any woman who grasps the "sweet ornament" of passion is in the process of becoming uncommonly beautiful.

> Life should not be a journey to the grave with the intention of arriving safely in an attractive and well preserved body, but rather a skid in broadside in a cloud of smoke, thoroughly used up, totally worn out, and loudly proclaiming, "Wow! What a Ride!"[14]
>
> HUNTER S. THOMPSON

Questions for Reflection and Discussion

1. Do you agree that passion can make a woman uncommonly beautiful? Why or why not?

2. When you think about passion, what qualities come to mind?

3. What stereotypes does our culture give us of passion?

4. In your experience, who models or has modeled passion for you?

5. In what ways do other people consider you to be a passionate woman?

6. In what ways would you like to become a passionate woman?

7. What steps can you take to nurture passion in your life?

CHAPTER 2 *Wisdom*

Never mistake knowledge for wisdom. One helps you make a living; the other helps you make a life.[1]

SANDRA CAREY

My grandmother attended school only through the third grade, but she is the wisest woman I have known. In the piney woods of Louisiana in the early 1900s, my grandmother's life consisted of gardening, raising chickens, and cooking and cleaning for her large family. Married at fourteen, she gave birth to fifteen children, raised the thirteen who survived infancy, and was dearly beloved by her thirty-five grandchildren. To me it was her wisdom—

her common sense, sound judgment, and discretion—
that helped her "make a life."

Her wisdom was exemplified by her forthrightness
and sense of humor. She once said about her children,
"I wouldn't take a zillion dollars for any one of them or
pay a nickel for another one." Late in my grandmother's life, one of my cousins called her and asked how
old she was when she married our grandfather. A few
minutes after my cousin hung up the phone, Grandma
called my cousin back and announced, "And I didn't
have to either!" and then hung up. When I was expe-
riencing morning sickness with my first pregnancy, I
went to visit her. I told her how I was feeling, and she
responded, "There's not much I don't know about that
disease!"

Grandma was the epitome of discretion. When
asked about someone, she would answer honestly, but
she never spoke in an unkind way or tried to interfere.
I remember her saying, "If I had that problem, I think
I would get busy and do something about it." Along
with her discretion, she had an innate ability to make
each one of us feel special. She was amazingly impartial,
and all of us agree that she had no favorites.

But it was my grandmother's common sense that

affected me the most. After my grandfather's funeral,
she met with the family and shared a couple of ground
rules for the future. Everyone was welcome to visit
anytime—the door was always open—but she didn't want
any of her children or grandchildren living with her,
and she was not available to babysit! In her wisdom she
knew that if she was to maintain her sanity and impar-
tiality, then her family
needed to honor these
desires.

    My grandmother
was wise, for she knew

Main Entry: wis-dom
Pronunciation: 'wiz-dəm
a: knowledge **b**: insight **c**: good sense
d: judgment **e**: a wise attitude or course
of action

her limitations, and she knew what she needed to do to
maintain family unity. Although she probably did not
know the dictionary definition of *wisdom,* she embodied
this virtue. She skillfully used knowledge to make good
decisions and to "make a life." My grandmother was
not a beauty, but she was beautiful. Her wisdom made
her so.

    When I was a young girl, the word *wisdom* was
usually applied to someone who was considered a
"brain." The profile of a smart girl was one who wore
glasses, stayed home every night, and studied all the
time. Wisdom was associated with someone who was

not fun, had little personality, and was not considered to be attractive. Wisdom was equated with the pursuit of knowledge. But as Sandra Carey reminds us, we are not to confuse the two—wisdom is applying knowledge in order to live sensibly.

I think that wisdom is a great beautifier. A woman who practices discernment and sound judgment is attractive. My friend Lois is like that. She truly listens, thinks, and then speaks. She usually asks a few questions and then shares a wise insight. She is confident, settled within herself, and positive in her outlook. It is her wisdom that enables her to be quiet before she speaks. Lois illustrates the truth of the adage "Knowledge talks, wisdom listens." Lois is the picture of discretion.

In contrast to the fragrance of Lois's quiet beauty was the scent of foolishness and indiscretion I experienced recently. I was at the mall, sitting next to a group of teenage girls who were having a snack. Their conversation was loud, boisterous, and regrettably profane. Although the girls were cute and well-dressed, their coarse speech sullied their physical beauty. As I observed these young girls, I thought of the words of the wise King Solomon: "A beautiful woman who lacks discretion is like a gold ring in a pig's snout."[2]

An attractive woman who lacks discretion or wisdom can actually mar her loveliness. Yet an "unattractive" woman who is wise can be considered beautiful.

> *For wisdom is far more valuable than rubies. Nothing you desire can compare with it.*[3]

KING SOLOMON

Her Wisdom Transformed Society

Florence Nightingale prized wisdom in order to make a life that was more valuable than rubies. Well-educated by her wealthy father, Florence was brilliant, charming, and independent. Her father liked for her to read aloud to him from a Victorian book of manners titled *Passages in the Life of a Daughter at Home.* However, Florence's preference for personal reading was *The Annual Report of the Fliedner Institute*—a report of a German training school for nurses. Her burning desire was to get away from the superficiality of society and be involved with the poor and those who suffered. When she announced that she wanted to become a nurse, her family was stunned and horrified. Nurses of that day were considered to be menial laborers and were often women of questionable morals.

But Florence was determined. She studied anatomy and visited the county hospital. On a trip to Germany, she spent two weeks at the Fliedner Nursing School, and in 1851 she received three months of nurses' training at Kaiserswerth, a German school and hospital. This training qualified her to be the superintendent of the "Establishment for Gentlewomen during Illness." There she scrubbed floors, bandaged wounds, and brought hope.

During the Crimean War, the British government commissioned a company of volunteer nurses, mostly from religious orders, to serve in a makeshift hospital in Scutari, Turkey. Organized and led by Florence, these dedicated women unflinchingly faced the daunting task of improving conditions and ministering to the sick. Florence found the wounded soldiers in a ruined barracks that had no medical supplies, no kitchen, no running water, no beds—only an abundance of rats. Because of the deplorable conditions, the death rate was exceptionally high. She immediately requested two hundred scrub brushes.

It was Florence's wisdom that enabled her to revolutionize health care and to establish nursing as a valued profession. It was her common sense that prompted her to ask for scrub brushes. It was her sound judgment that made her realize that the hospital in Scutari was built on top of a sewer. After she insisted that it be drained and disinfected, the death rate dropped by 80 percent! It was her discernment that led her to isolate the patients who had contagious diseases. She applied her wisdom skillfully and practically by serving healthy food and providing clean bedding and clothes.

Often at the end of a twenty-hour day, Florence could be seen walking through the wards with a little lamp in her hand, ready to help if needed. The soldiers idolized her. Just her presence gave the men strength and hope.

Florence returned from the war a national hero, but sadly her own health had deteriorated, and she was incapacitated for the rest of her life. Although she was physically limited, she passionately campaigned for medical and public health reform, established the Nightingale Home for the training of nurses, and wrote *Notes on Nursing,* a classic book on nursing.

Her modesty kept her from making public appearances or granting interviews. Her focus was not on herself or her accomplishments; her focus was on the great need for transforming the medical community.

Florence Nightingale was indeed a wise woman.

> *Miss Nightingale did inspire awe, not because one felt afraid of her per se, but because the very essence of Truth seemed to emanate from her, and because of her perfect fearlessness in telling it.*[4]
>
> WILLIAM RICHMOND

Her Wisdom Saved Thousands of Lives

If you were to think of literary heroines who were wise, I doubt that the name Scheherazade would be on the top of your list. But the more I learned about this woman, the more I admired her incredible discernment and judgment.

When I was a young girl, I was fascinated by the stories about Aladdin and his magic lamp, the voyages of Sinbad, and, of course, Ali Baba and the forty thieves. You probably remember the password the leader of the thieves used to open a cave full of gold and jewel: *Open, Sesame!* Ali Baba's story is only one of hundreds of captivating stories found in a thirty-volume series entitled *The Stories of the Thousand Nights and a Night,* also known as *Stories from the Thousand and One Nights.* How these fables came into being is the best fairy tale of all.

One day King Shahryar was shocked to discover that his wife was unfaithful to him. Her duplicity was such a staggering betrayal that he had her killed. He resolutely swore by the "Raiser of the Heavens" that from then on, he would marry a virgin at night, sleep with her, and then have her beheaded the next morning.

This horrific scenario was well into its third year when Scheherazade, oldest daughter of the king's prime minister, approached her father with a plan. Because of her father's position in the kingdom, she and her sister were exempted from the king's edict. But Scheherazade was not only distressed at King Shahryar's actions but also committed to doing what she could to end this slaughter.

Scheherazade was a most knowledgeable woman. She had read "the books, annals, and legends of preceding kings, and the stories, examples, and instances of bygone men and things. Indeed it was said that she had collected a thousand books of histories relating to antique races and departed rulers. She had perused the works of the poets and knew them by heart. She had studied philosophy and the sciences, arts, and accomplishments. And she was pleasant and polite, wise and witty, well read and well bred."[5]

But this young woman was more than knowledgeable. She knew what to do with her knowledge.

She was wise. Scheherazade approached her father and asked that he give her in marriage to the king. The prime minister was distraught, and he blamed and reproached her for addressing him "in words so wide from wisdom and unfar from foolishness." She was determined, though, to "save both sides from destruction."[6]

Before Scheherazade was presented to the king, she instructed her sister, Dunyazade, to come to her when summoned and say, "O my sister, an thou be not sleepy, relate to me some new story, delectable and delightsome, the better to speed our waking hours."[7]

At midnight, Scheherazade called for her sister, who then loudly asked Scheherazade to tell her a story. The king, who had been unable to sleep, heard the request and was himself eager to be entertained. He gave Scheherazade permission to tell a story.

So began the continuous stories of this creative young woman. For nearly three years—a thousand and one nights—Scheherazade drew from her well of knowledge and wove tales that would distract this vindictive king. Her plan was to tell stories that would so captivate the king that, wanting more stories, he would delay killing her. Each night, when she finished her story, she would say, "And yet, O King! this is not more wondrous than the story of . . ."[8] and she would tell him the title of the next tale. The king was so captivated by her storytelling that he let her live another day.

After a thousand nights and countless stories, Scheherazade asked to be exempt from the threat of death. The king gladly granted her request, and they lived together happily ever after.

She was one wise woman. She gathered all of her knowledge and used it to save her own life—and the lives of a thousand other young women who would have been killed by the murderous king.

> *It's their minds, in the end. It's what makes a woman beautiful when she's young, and it's what makes a woman beautiful when she is old.*[9]

CATE BLANCHETT

Her Wisdom Meant More than Money

Florence Nightingale and Scheherazade both diligently sought wisdom. They sacrificed and studied to gain wisdom so that they could "make a life." To become wise, we must desire to be wise.

Another woman who had an insatiable desire to be wise is the queen of Sheba, whom we learn about in the Bible.[10] We are told that she spent two and a half months traveling two thousand miles by camel across a scorching desert to get answers for some of the questions that burned in her heart. Would you be willing to endure that degree of discomfort in order to gain wisdom?

To become wise, we must desire to be wise.

The queen had heard stories about a wise and wealthy king who ruled Israel. Curious and inquisitive, she wanted to test the wisdom of the remarkable King Solomon. Her quest for knowledge prompted her to make the sacrifices of time and comfort.

The biblical account indicates that the queen of Sheba was a wealthy woman, yet apparently her riches did not satisfy her, did not help her "make a life." Solomon himself said, "How much better to get wisdom than gold, and good judgment than silver!"[11] She knew in her heart that the jewels she wore were inconsequential compared to the adornment of understanding and good judgment.

The queen was not disappointed in what she learned or saw. The Bible states, "When she met with Solomon, she talked with him about everything she had on her mind. Solomon had answers for all her questions; nothing was too hard for the king to explain to her. When the queen of Sheba realized how very wise Solomon was, and when she saw the palace he had built, she was overwhelmed."[12]

> *In seeking wisdom, thou art wise; in imagining that thou hast attained it, thou art a fool.*[13]
>
> BEN SIRA

Wisdom out of Balance

We have considered three women who treasured wisdom and who were able to use their knowledge to influence those around them for good. But some women irrationally make unwise choices and end up hurting others, often living with the irreversible consequences.

Such is the story of Rebekah, the wife of the Old Testament patriarch Isaac.[14] The first book of the Bible, Genesis, introduces us to this beautiful woman who was mother of twin boys, Esau and Jacob. Unlike my grandmother, Rebekah did not use good judgment; she played favorites and showed partiality toward her son Jacob.

It was customary for the father to give a blessing to the firstborn son. But when Rebekah overheard her husband tell their older twin, Esau, that he wanted to give him the blessing, she quickly planned for Jacob, her favorite, to deceive his father and fraudulently receive the blessing. When Jacob objected, Rebekah told him, "Let the curse fall on me, my son. . . . Just do what I tell you."[15]

Whenever I read this account, I think, *What was Rebekah thinking? Why was she compelled to ask her son to deceive? Did she even stop to think of the consequences of her actions?* Unfortunately Rebekah's world revolved solely around her favored son. She unwisely became obsessed with Jacob's position and success. She willingly sacrificed what was right, with no thought of the impact her deceit would have on her son and family. King Solomon would later write about women like Rebekah: "A wise woman builds her home, but a foolish woman tears it down with her own hands."[16]

A determined Rebekah unwisely forced her own son to lie to his father. As a result of her poor judgment, her family was divided. Jacob was forced to leave, and she never saw him again. Surely Esau and Isaac were also deeply hurt by her betrayal. "Wise people think before they act."[17] If only Rebekah had chosen to be wise.

> *To acquire knowledge, one must study; but to acquire wisdom, one must observe.*[18]
>
> MARILYN VOS SAVANT

Becoming a Wise Woman

I realize now that for many years I thought that wisdom was an inherited quality—we either have it or we don't. And I wasn't sure there was any good way to acquire it. How unwise of me!

Observation is a vital part of learning to be wise; that is why it is good to examine the lives of women who have gone before us. It is better to read about and learn from a Rebekah than to make the same mistakes ourselves.

In observing the lives of Florence Nightingale, Scheherazade, and the queen of Sheba, we find that each one was willing to search for wisdom. Florence visited hospitals, did research, and studied for several months at a German school and hospital. She gained

all the knowledge that she could and was ultimately able
to wisely put her knowledge into practice. Through
Scheherazade's extensive study, she was thoroughly
prepared to tell stories for a thousand and one nights!
She purposely set her heart to gain wisdom.

I so appreciate the example these women give us.
They inspire me to believe that if they could do it, so
can I.

When I was pregnant with our first child, I needed
all the help I could get. Because my husband was serving in the military overseas, I flew to Japan to join him.
But that meant I left behind all of my known support
system, all of the advice and hands-on help from family
or friends. In those days I had no e-mail access, no
Internet sources I could consult. Just how was I going to
handle this huge transition? Who would show me what
I needed to know? On some level I knew the truth of
what Antonio de Guevara wrote: "Among wise men, the
wisest knows that he knows least."[19] Knowing I needed
to gather knowledge, I enrolled in a Red Cross course
and devoured Dr. Spock's baby book. I went to the
library often to read other books. I knew that I needed
to acquire as much wisdom as I could.

The truly wise readily acknowledge the need for

wisdom. Julie's husband had always taken care of their finances. He died suddenly, leaving her with an extensive stock portfolio. She felt totally inadequate to handle this new responsibility. What was she to do? She bought several books about financial investing, and she enrolled in a class to learn more about the stock market and wise use of money. Julie actively sought the knowledge she needed to make good financial decisions.

In his writings about biblical proverbs, John Phillips tells us, "Wisdom is as available today as it was in Solomon's time. Flood tides of books, newspapers, and magazines pour daily from printing presses. . . . Schools, colleges, and universities beckon. Libraries bulge with resources. Pulpits, law courts, and the halls of government instruct and inform. Wisdom can be found everywhere, although we often need to separate it from a great deal of accompanying folly."[20]

We can acquire wisdom, and we don't have to make a two-thousand-mile trip to gain it. We can take classes, read books, and search the Internet to gain knowledge in order to make wise choices.

We can also spend time with wise people. The queen of Sheba understood this principle: "Become wise by walking with the wise."[21] We can do the same.

Who are the wise women in your life? Are they are your friends or family members? Are they the women whose books you have read? Choose friends who are committed to living wisely. Spend time with them. Ask them questions. Learn from their lives— from their mistakes as well as their successes.

Spend time with wise people.

Seek out women who will mentor you. I have never forgotten the many jewels of wisdom my mentor, Mary, passed on to me. Mary once told me, "If you don't learn to bend and be flexible, then you will break." I also learned this truth by observing my grandmother. She never said, "Sometimes you need to go with the flow," but she lived out that truth in front of my eyes.

For me, wisdom is the bedrock quality of inner beauty, for without it all the other qualities could easily become unbalanced. Wisdom keeps us from making impulsive, foolish choices. It adorns our spirit as no other, and it enables us to make a life—a full and blessed one. "For Wisdom is better than all the trap-

pings of wealth; nothing you could wish for holds a
candle to her."[22]

> Never walk away from Wisdom—she guards your life;
>   love her—she keeps her eye on you.
> Above all and before all, do this: Get Wisdom!
>   Write this at the top of your list: Get Understanding!
> Throw your arms around her—believe me, you won't regret it;
>   never let her go—she'll make your life glorious.
> She'll garland your life with grace,
>   she'll festoon your days with beauty.[23]

KING SOLOMON

Questions for Reflection and Discussion

1. How would you describe a wise woman?

2. What stereotypes does our culture give us of wisdom?

3. In your experience, who models or has modeled wisdom for you?

4. In what ways do other people consider you to be gracious? a wise woman?

5. In what ways would you like to become a wise woman?

6. What steps can you take to nurture wisdom in your life?

CHAPTER 3 *Integrity*

*Character contributes to beauty.
It fortifies a woman as her youth
fades. A mode of conduct, a
standard of courage, discipline,
fortitude and integrity can do a
great deal to make a woman
beautiful.*[1]

JACQUELINE BISSET

I hurriedly unloaded my bags of groceries into
the car, dutifully returned the cart to its designat-
ed place, and drove home. After putting away the
groceries, I went to get my calendar out of my purse,
but my purse wasn't in its usual place! Wondering if
I had left it in the car, I checked, but it wasn't there.
As I thought about where it might be, I panicked. It

dawned on me that I had left it in the grocery cart in the parking lot.

I jumped in the car and drove quickly back to the store. All I could think of as I drove was all of the essentials that were in my purse—credit cards, calendar, phone, money. When I arrived back at the store, I ran to the front doors, looking at the carts—they were all empty. With my heart beating rapidly and I'm sure with desperation written on my face, I asked the customer service representative if anyone had turned in a purse.

The man smiled and said that some Good Samaritan had found my purse, brought it to him, and said that she knew I would be frantic! I was incredibly relieved. If only I could have thanked and hugged the woman—this beautiful woman who was honest and conscientious.

I agree with Jacqueline Bisset: Integrity can do a great deal to make a woman beautiful. Maybe you've had an experience like mine, where someone's honesty saved the day for you. Or maybe you know a woman who was willing to stand her ground for what was right, even in the face of great pressure. Women of integrity are not only beautiful, they shine. Their radiance reflects a purity of heart that can only be called beautiful.

When I think about a woman of integrity, I think about her honesty, her sensitive conscience that makes her committed to doing what is right and honorable. A woman of integrity is trustworthy, responsible, and truthful. The woman who found my purse did not think twice about returning it. She knew it was the right thing to do, and she did it. She was beautiful!

Someone who does not possess integrity is untrustworthy, dishonest, unfaith-

Main Entry: in-teg-ri-ty
Pronunciation: in-'te-grə-tē
a: honesty **b**: firm adherence to a code of values **c**: incorruptibility **d**: state of being complete, undivided

ful, and deceptive—unattractive qualities to say the least. I have a friend whose purse was stolen, and it was eventually found in a trash bin, but all of her valuables were missing. The person who took her handbag was not honorable and, in my estimation, certainly not attractive.

Integrity is an essential quality of inner beauty. The women whom we will discuss in this chapter were willing to make hard choices about a right course of action, and their choices have shaped our world. We are drawn to women whom we can trust and who have a strong sense of right and wrong.

True to Her Values

On a December night in 1955, Rosa Parks rode a
bus home after a day of work at the Montgomery Fair
department store. Her thoughts were occupied with the
things she needed to do when she got home—prepare
a workshop for teenagers and send out notices for the
election of officers for the National Association for the
Advancement of Colored People. She served as secretary
for the Montgomery, Alabama, chapter of the NAACP
and worked hard for the rights of black citizens in the
racially segregated South.

In those days, the buses were divided into separate sections for blacks and whites: the white section in
the front, and the "colored" section in the back. Black
people could sit in the middle of the bus until the white
section was full; then they had to move to the back of
the bus, or if there was no room, they were expected to
leave the bus.

That night Rosa sat in the first row behind the
white section of the bus. However, when a white
man boarded the bus and found no seats available
in the white section, the bus driver asked Rosa and
the three other black people in that row to move. All

but Rosa got up and took seats in the back of the bus. She refused and just moved over and sat by the window.

In recalling the incident for *Eyes on the Prize*, a 1987 public television series on the civil rights movement, Rosa said, "When [the bus driver] saw me still sitting, he asked if I was going to stand up, and I said, 'No, I'm not.' He said, 'Well, if you don't stand up, I'm going to have to call the police and have you arrested.' I said, 'You may do that.'"[2]

The bus driver called the police, who arrested Rosa and took her to jail. She was later found guilty of disorderly conduct and violating a local ordinance.

It was Rosa's integrity, her firm adherence to a code of values, that prompted her not to move from her seat. In her autobiography, *My Story*, Rosa tells of her motivation for her action. "People always say that I didn't give up my seat because I was tired, but that isn't true. I was not tired physically, or no more tired than I usually was at the end of a working day. I was not old, although some people have an image of me as being old then. I was forty-two. No, the only tired I was, was tired of giving in."[3]

It was Rosa's integrity that emboldened her to stand firm in the face of injustice. It was her integrity that told her discrimination and inequality were worth fighting against. It was her integrity that said, "Enough."

Although Rosa's story begins with a grave injustice, it ends with a hard-fought victory for equality. Rosa Parks's quiet defiance on that winter evening "was the spark that ignited the demonstrations of the 1950s and the 1960s. Because of her action, segregation laws were eventually struck down, Martin Luther King Jr. emerged as a national leader, and a long struggle for racial equality was engaged with renewed fervor."[4] Congress referred to Rosa as the mother of the modern-day civil rights movement. Rosa's actions led to eventual racial integration in the South.

When Rosa was eighty-three years old, she was awarded the Presidential Medal of Freedom and the Congressional Gold Medal. After she died, her body was laid in state in the Capitol Rotunda—the first woman ever to receive that honor. Fifty thousand people viewed her casket. Her funeral lasted seven hours, and three presidents spoke in her honor. By presidential order, flags were flown at half-staff on the day of her internment—an incredible finale for a black seamstress with only a high school education. A fitting tribute to a beautiful woman of integrity.

This above all—to thine own self be true,
And it must follow, as the night the day,
Thou canst not then be false to any man.[5]

HAMLET

True to Her Principles

Jane Eyre is one of my favorite literary heroines. I've
not only read the book *Jane Eyre,* but I've also watched
every film version of the classic novel. Charlotte Brontë
vividly portrays the triumphant spirit of the orphaned
Jane in her pursuit for independence and a sense of
being valued. I am drawn to Jane because of her indom-
itable spirit and the integrity she exercised at crucial
times in her life. Jane Eyre was true to her principles.

Sent from the home of her cruel aunt to live
in harsh conditions in a girls' school, Jane excelled
academically despite the hardships and eventually
became a teacher. As a result of an ad in the newspaper,
she traveled to Thornfield Manor, where she was hired
to tutor Adele, the ward of the manor's master, Mr.
Rochester. A moody, stern middle-aged man, Rochester
was drawn to the plain yet spirited Jane Eyre. In fact, he
fell in love with her and eventually proposed marriage.
Jane joyfully accepted and eagerly awaited the wedding

day. However, just as Rochester and Jane were to take
their vows, the wedding was interrupted and cancelled
when a lawyer rushed into the church and proclaimed
that the wedding could not proceed. When the minister asked why, the man announced that Rochester was
already married! Distraught, Rochester took the wedding
party to the third floor of his manor to see Bertha
Mason, the insane woman who was still legally his wife.

Rochester begged Jane to stay with him, even
though his wife was still alive. In his eyes, he was not
truly married. He asked Jane to forgive him, declaring
his eternal love for her. He tried to convince her that
because they loved each other, it was only right that they
stay together.

Jane wrestled with her conscience. She deeply
loved Rochester. Should she overlook his legal standing
with his wife? Should she stay at Thornfield Manor and
continue her relationship to him?

The temptation to stay was overwhelming. Her
reason urged her, "Oh, comply! . . . Think of his
misery; think of his danger when left alone . . . soothe
him; save him; love him; tell him you love him and will
be his. Who in the world cares for you? or who will be
injured by what you do?"[6]

However, when Jane looked inside, when she considered her own principles, she stood firm: "I care for myself. The more solitary, the more friendless, the more unsustained I am, the more I will respect myself. I will keep the law given by God; sanctioned by man. I will hold to the principles received by me when I was sane, and not mad—as I am now. Laws and principles are not for the times when there is no temptation; they are for such moments as this, when body and soul rise in mutiny against their rigour; stringent are they; inviolate they shall be. If at my individual convenience I might break them, what would be their worth?"[7]

Because of her integrity, Jane was confident of her own worth and knew she could not compromise herself, for if she did, she would lose her dignity and her self-respect. She believed that principles are worth nothing if they can be violated at will. Principles are for "such moments as this."

She believed that principles are worth nothing if they can be violated at will.

Resolutely Jane sacrificed her feelings and longings. She left Thornfield brokenhearted but with certainty in her heart that what she was doing was right.

After an agonizing and difficult journey, Jane was taken in and cared for by St. John Rivers and his sisters. Asked by the austere and controlling St. John to accompany him to India as his wife, Jane was again challenged to be true to herself.

Jane consented to go to India as his sister, his companion, but she declined his offer of marriage. She knew there would be no closeness or understanding in their relationship. She thought, "But as his wife—at his side always, and always restrained, and always checked—forced to keep the fire of my nature continually low, to compel it to burn inwardly and never utter a cry, though the imprisoned flame consumed vital after vital—*this* would be unendurable."[8] Jane was not willing to settle for a relationship of convenience.

In the end, Jane returned to Thornfield Manor, which she found in ruins from a fire started by Bertha Mason. When Jane found Rochester, she saw a desolate man, blinded and crippled in a hopeless effort to save his wife. He was overcome with joy at her return. They expressed their undying love for each other and were married three days later.

As we look back over Jane's life, we find that because she was deeply committed to truth, she did not consent to Rochester's pressure to choose passion over principle, and she did not succumb to St. John's demand to choose principle without passion. When Jane returned to Rochester, she was secure in who she was and was confident in where she belonged. She returned freely, as ready to give as she was to receive. She returned as a strong, trustworthy, beautiful woman because of her integrity.

> *Don't compromise yourself. You are all you've got.*[9]
> JANIS JOPLIN

True to Her Convictions

I defined a woman of integrity as being trustworthy, responsible, and truthful. This definition perfectly describes Abigail, a woman we learn about in the Old Testament.[10] In describing Abigail and her husband, Nabal, the Bible says, "Abigail was a sensible and beautiful woman. But Nabal . . . was mean and dishonest in all his dealings."[11]

Nabal's meanness was evident in his dealings with David, a successful military general and the man

anointed to be the next king of Israel. One day during
the season when Nabal's men were shearing his thou-
sands of sheep and goats, David sent a messenger to ask
Nabal for some provisions of food. It was a reasonable
request. David and his men had protected Nabal's flocks
from marauders, and now they were hungry and needed sustenance. David knew that the wealthy landowner
could spare the food. However, Nabal refused, dug in
his heels, and responded rudely to David's request, calling him and his men outlaws.

Greatly offended by Nabal's brusque and disre-
spectful response, David gathered his men to seek
retribution, planning to kill Nabal and all the men of
his household. One of Nabal's servants learned of the
plan and went to Abigail. The servant told Abigail that
David's men did not deserve her husband's contempt,
that David and his men had protected Nabal's flocks,
bringing only good to her husband.

Abigail immediately understood the situation and
knew that she must do something to avert disaster. She
quickly loaded donkeys with bread, wine, grain, cakes,
and meat. She intercepted David and pled with him,
falling at his feet and saying, "I accept all blame in this
matter, my lord. . . . I know Nabal is a wicked and ill-

tempered man; please don't pay any attention to him. He is a fool, just as his name suggests. But I never even saw the young men you sent."[12]

I have always appreciated Abigail's total honesty about her husband. She did not hide the truth. She did not try to excuse her husband or lie to protect him. She was straightforward with David and true to herself.

Abigail was a faithful wife, yet she was ready to act independently in her willingness to protect both her husband and their household. Her strong sense of doing what was right compelled her to intercede on Nabal's behalf, something only a woman of integrity would do.

She didn't allow her circumstances to dictate her character.

Abigail's commitment to be true to herself has always challenged me. She was in a difficult marriage, which probably in those days was arranged, but she didn't allow her circumstances to dictate her character. She was realistic, transparent, and genuine.

When she told her husband what she had done,

he had a stroke. Ten days later he died. When David learned of Nabal's death, he asked Abigail to become his wife. What a fitting reward for her sincerity and conscientiousness.

> *People with integrity have firm footing.*[13]
>
> KING SOLOMON

Lack of Integrity

Just as integrity makes a woman beautiful, the lack of integrity robs a woman of beauty. The Bible tells the story of Potiphar's wife.[14] We don't know if she was physically beautiful, but her character was certainly not.

She and her husband, the captain of the guard for the ruling pharaoh, lived in Egypt centuries ago. Potiphar bought a Hebrew slave, Joseph, to serve in his household. Joseph did an outstanding job and earned many promotions; eventually Potiphar asked Joseph to manage his entire household. Potiphar's wife was attracted to the handsome young slave and found ways to be near him. She often tried to seduce him.

One day when she and Joseph were alone, she grabbed his shirt and once again insisted that he sleep with her. He refused her advances, and sensing her determination, he ran from the room. But when he did, his shirt came off in her hand.

Rebuffed and scorned, she lied to cover herself: "My husband has brought this Hebrew slave here to insult us! . . . He tried to rape me, but I screamed. When he heard my loud cries, he ran and left his shirt behind with me." She took the shirt to her husband and told him, "That Hebrew slave you've had around here tried to make a fool of me," she said. "I was saved only by my screams."[15] Believing his wife's claims, Potiphar threw Joseph, an innocent man, into prison.

How could Potiphar's wife so willingly compromise her marriage, so willingly lie, and so willingly send an innocent person to prison? She was dishonest, unfaithful, and deceptive. Surely she did not sleep well at night, and certainly her lack of integrity would have made her countenance hard and cold.

Becoming a Woman of Integrity

Whether Rosa Parks or Abigail realized it at the time, they stood on firm ground in the midst of their trials because of their integrity. They were sustained by knowing that they made the right choice.

I was deeply moved by the story I heard of a young couple who were engaged to be married. Several months before the wedding, the groom-to-be was diagnosed with an incurable cancer. He had, at the most, two years to live. He released his fiancée, Margaret, from her commitment to marry him, not wanting her to suffer or be bound to someone who was dying. But Margaret insisted that the wedding take place immediately so that they could have as much time together as possible. Her loyalty and faithfulness validated her integrity—she was willing to keep her commitment even when the circumstances changed. Margaret stood on solid ground.

Julia also demonstrated integrity. In her late twenties, Julia graduated with two master's degrees—one in law and one in theology—from a prominent graduate school in the East. Because of her high level of competence and stellar academic record, Julia was inundated with job offers, many of them from prestigious law firms around the country. But when she was just weeks away from taking the bar exam, she decided to withdraw from the process. Through prayer, she realized that her passion was with ministry, not law. The problem was, she had no job offers in ministry. But rather than

take the bar exam and head into a lucrative law career
for which she had no passion, she opted to wait. Even
though Julia didn't know what the future held, she was
committed to staying true to her principles.

The quality of being undivided and adhering to
a code of values is a choice for each individual. The
woman who found my purse made a choice to return
it. Rosa Parks chose not to give up her seat on the bus.
Jane Eyre chose to leave Thornfield rather than stay
in a relationship with a married man. Abigail chose
to intercede on her husband's behalf. Margaret chose
to marry a dying man. Julia chose to refuse lucrative
job offers. And Potiphar's wife chose to deceive.

Integrity is a choice.

Harper Lee observed, "The one thing that doesn't
abide by majority rule is a person's conscience."[16] Each
of us must decide how we will respond when we are
faced with challenges to our own code of values.

On a recent return flight from an overseas trip
with my husband, I was filling out our customs form.
I realized that because of some gifts we had bought, we
would be a little over the prescribed amount to enter

the country without paying duty. The last thing I wanted to do was to go through the complications of paying
duty for our gifts, but if I was to be faithful to my code
of values, then I needed to put down the correct price
for everything we had purchased. And I did. When I
handed our form to the customs agent, he looked at
it, then at us, and waved us through. I was relieved and
thankful that I had maintained my integrity.

Sometimes integrity demands that we admit our
wrongs. Anne Morrow Lindbergh demonstrated her
integrity by publicly admitting a mistake she made.
Anne was the wife of Charles Lindbergh and was
herself a pioneering aviator and author. In 1940 she
wrote a book entitled *The Wave of the Future,* in which
she wrote favorably about Nazi Germany. Later, in
1973, she admitted, "It was a mistake. . . . It didn't
help anybody. . . . I didn't have the right to write it. I
didn't know enough."[17] It takes a woman of integrity to
acknowledge her faults.

> *Integrity is attractive because truth*
> *bestows a loveliness that*
> *is rarely found.*

Each of us can be a woman of integrity. All we need to do is carefully choose our code of values and be true to ourselves. Integrity graces its bearer with a settled assurance of who we are and what we believe. Integrity is attractive because truth bestows a loveliness that is rarely found. Character does contribute to beauty—and integrity can do a great deal to make a woman beautiful. Uncommonly beautiful.

> *The willingness to accept responsibility for one's own life is the source from which self~respect springs.*[18]
>
> JOAN DIDION

Questions for Reflection and Discussion

1. How would you describe a woman of integrity?

2. What does our culture teach us about integrity?

3. In your experience, who models or has modeled integrity for you?

4. In what ways do other people consider you to be a woman of integrity?

5. In what ways would you like to become a woman of integrity?

6. What steps can you take to nurture integrity in your life?

CHAPTER 4 *Selflessness*

*It is only in the giving of oneself
to others that we truly live.*[1]

ETHEL PERCY ANDRUS

My morning began with an early departure to the downtown courthouse to report for jury duty. By noon I had connected with a friend, Lucille, whom I had not seen for a while, and we agreed to have lunch together. I told Lucille that we could go to the nearby sandwich shop to eat. Lucille placed her hand on mine and said, "Cynthia, that won't be necessary. This morning I made two lunches. I didn't know who I would be eating lunch with, a friend or a stranger, but apparently my extra lunch is for you!"

I have never forgotten this incident because I

was so touched by Lucille's consideration for others. I feel I am being kind when I prepare a meal for someone I know I will see. I don't think I've ever thought of doing something extra for someone I *might* encounter.

Lucille is a living illustration of selflessness. I don't think Lucille thought twice about packing an extra lunch. It was a natural choice for her to give to others in small and surprising ways—even to an old acquaintance at a courthouse.

Selflessness often expresses itself in self-sacrificing acts and sometimes in heroic acts. The women we will look at in this chapter all had more concern for others than they did for themselves.

Selflessness That Saved Children's Lives

Amy Carmichael was an unlikely candidate to be an activist. Born in 1867, she left her home country of England to go to India as a missionary. Despite a debilitating illness that often left her bedridden for months, Amy actively practiced her calling: rescuing young children from sex trafficking. Hardly a job for the weak.

Once in India, Amy soon became aware that young girls were brought to Hindu temples and forced to become prostitutes to earn money for the priests.

Appalled by the neglect and abuse she saw, she devoted her life to rescuing these children. She began the Dohnavur Fellowship, which cared for more than a thousand temple children. Although saving the children was risky and exhausting work, Amy was compelled by God's love to provide a sanctuary where they could grow up in an atmosphere of love.

Main Entry: self-less-ness
Pronunciation: 'sel-fləs-nəs
a: having no concern for self **b**: unselfish **c**: acting with less concern for yourself than for the success of the joint activity **d**: self-sacrificing

Amy Carmichael's selflessness was not without cost. The work took its toll on her body, and it often put her life in danger. People criticized her, saying that all she was doing was babysitting. *So be it,* Amy thought. *If I can spare the lives of these precious children, I will be a nursemaid.*[2] She never tried to make a name for herself. Although Amy never married, she was never alone. She carried with her a promise from God, "None of them that trust in him shall be desolate."[3]

Amy lived not for herself, but for others. A verse that she asked others to pray for her was, He "made himself of no reputation, and took upon him the form of a servant."[4] Her prayer was "that I may get down to the bottom of that verse."[5]

I think that Amy did get down to the bottom of
that verse. She served in India for fifty-five years until
her death, leaving a role model of a woman whose selflessness made her beautiful.

Another woman whose selflessness had an enor-
mous impact on the lives of children was Henrietta
Szold. I first heard about this amazing woman when
I toured Jerusalem. She was known for establishing
a Zionist volunteer organization for women, Hadas-
sah, which provided medical care and education to the
Jewish community in Palestine.

In the 1930s, burdened by the needs of young
children during the impending Holocaust, Henrietta
not only secured visas and transportation for eleven
thousand children but also established an educational
and support system for them. She tried to meet every
arriving transport and took a personal interest in the
placement and care of each child.

Henrietta was named "Mother of the Yishuv" (the
Jewish community in Palestine) and was also nominat-
ed for the Nobel Prize. She downplayed her qualities
by saying she was just a "hard worker." When she was
seventy-five years old, she noted that her greatest assets
were "'a strong constitution, a devotion to duty, and a

big conscience,' together with a 'flair for organization' and 'a pretty big capacity for righteous indignation.'"[6] Sounds like good attributes for a selfless woman.

> *You can give without loving. But you cannot love without giving.*[7]
> AMY CARMICHAEL

Selfless Expressions of Love

Della Dillingham Young personified Amy Carmichael's words about the compelling nature of love to give. Generations of readers have been touched by the wonderful short story *The Gift of the Magi* by the writer whose pen name was O. Henry.

It was the day before Christmas, and Della and her husband, Jim, were just a stone's throw away from poverty. Each wanted to give the other a special gift, but the couple had almost no money. Each, however, had something of value: Jim had a gold watch he had inherited from his father and grandfather; Della had thick, long, lovely hair. O. Henry describes these treasures: "Had the Queen of Sheba lived in the flat across the airshaft, Della would have let her hair hang out the window some day to dry just to depreciate Her Majesty's jewels and gifts. Had King Solomon been the janitor, with all his treasures piled up in the basement, Jim would have pulled out his watch every time he passed, just to see him pluck at his beard from envy."[8]

Thinking of the joy a special gift would bring her husband, Della sold her beautiful hair for twenty dollars and bought Jim a platinum chain for his watch. In an ironic twist, Jim sold his watch to buy an exquisite set of combs for Della's hair.

When Jim walked in and saw Della's short hair, she commented, "Maybe the hairs of my head were numbered, but nobody could ever count my love for you."[9] O. Henry observes, "I have lamely related to you the uneventful chronicle of two foolish children in a flat who most unwisely sacrificed for each other the greatest treasures of their house. But in a last word to the wise of these days let it be said that of all who give gifts, these two were the wisest. Of all who give and receive gifts, such as they are wisest. Everywhere they are wisest. They are the magi."[10] Della's and Jim's selflessness truly did make them the wisest.

Life lived just to satisfy yourself never satisfies anybody.[11]

UNKNOWN

Selflessness That Improved the Lives of Thousands

Blind at age five and abandoned to an orphanage at age ten, Anne Sullivan did not allow her circumstances to limit her. She longed to go to school and was eventually sent by a charity to the Perkins Institute for the Blind. After a series of surgeries, Anne regained her sight and went on to become the valedictorian of her class.

In 1887 the Institute sent Anne to the home of Helen Keller, a six-year-old who had been left blind and deaf by an attack of scarlet fever. Because of Anne's own experience, she was undaunted by the rebellious Helen and committed herself to helping Helen find a way out of her lonely, dark tunnel and communicate with the world around her. With extreme patience, Anne began by spelling out words on Helen's hands. From this small beginning, Anne's student was able to learn. Helen later enrolled at classes at Radcliffe College, where Anne attended classes with her and faithfully interpreted the lectures. The women's persistence was rewarded when Helen graduated *cum laude.*

Anne Sullivan's selflessness had a profound impact. As a result of her teaching and influence,

Helen Keller spent her life writing, lecturing, and raising funds on behalf of the blind. Anne did not live to satisfy herself; she literally created a life for someone else.

Often selflessness can be considered its own reward, but in Anne's case, she is also recognized along with Helen Keller as one of the great women of history. Without Anne's perseverance, inspiration, and selfless devotion, Helen never would have achieved her full potential. Helen later said of Anne Sullivan, "How much of my delight in all beautiful things is innate and how much is due to her influence, I can never tell. I feel that her being is inseparable from my own, and that the footsteps of my life are in hers. . . . There is not a talent or an aspiration or a joy in me that has not been awakened by her loving touch."[12]

> *I find life an exciting business, and most exciting when it is lived for others.*[13]
>
> HELEN KELLER

Selflessness That Saved a Race of People

How would you like to enjoy a twelve-month stay at a spa? The Bible tells us that this was Esther's experi-

ence. She spent a year at a spa in the court of King
Xerxes, where the most beautiful virgins in the
Persian Empire were indulged in lavish beauty treatments: six months with oil of myrrh, followed by six
months with special perfumes and ointments. The
purpose? One of the virgins would be chosen to be
the new queen.

Thrust into this unique beauty pageant was
Esther, a lovely young Jewish orphan.[14] Adopted by
her uncle Mordecai, Esther was cautioned by him not
to reveal her nationality to the people around her.
When the day finally arrived for Esther to be presented
to the king, he was overcome by her beauty and immediately set the royal crown on her head.

Trouble brewed when Haman, the king's prime
minister, had a run-in with Mordecai. When Haman
traveled through the kingdom, he expected people to
bow to him. However, Mordecai refused to bow to the
man, arousing Haman's anger. When the vindictive
Haman learned that Mordecai was a Jew, the prime
minister asked the king to decree that all Jews living
in Persia should be killed.

Mordecai begged Esther to go before the king
and plead their case. Esther's response is recorded in

the Bible: "The whole world knows that anyone who appears before the king in his inner court without being invited is doomed to die unless the king holds out his gold scepter. And the king has not called for me to come to him in more than a month."[15]

Mordecai reminded Esther that she, too, was a Jew and that perhaps she had been placed in the position as queen of Persia for such a time as this. Esther considered her uncle's request and decided to put aside her own desires and to advocate for her people. She asked all of the Jews in the town to fast on her behalf for three days. After that, she promised, "Then, though it is against the law, I will go in to see the king. If I must die, I am willing to die."[16]

These are incredible, courageous words of selflessness. Queen Esther was willing to risk her life in order to intercede for her people. In choosing to sacrifice herself, she became a living example of unselfish concern for the welfare of others. Aware of her opportunity to serve, she prepared herself and acted selflessly.

Like all good stories, this one has a happy ending. Esther and the Jews were spared, and she is forever remembered as a woman of selflessness and courage.

*To give without any reward, or any notice, has a special quality of
its own.*[17]

ANNE MORROW LINDBERGH

Selflessness out of Balance

Does selflessness require that we give ourselves entirely
away? The word by its nature seems to preclude any
thought of self. But I think a truly selfless woman is one
who does think of herself—in the right way. It is important to maintain a healthy balance between giving without thought for our own needs and recognizing that we
have legitimate needs.

Jennifer was constantly preparing meals for people
who were sick or struggling in some way. People recognized her as the generous one who always responded to
a need. However, no one knew what price her family
paid for her seemingly relentless service. She was often
so preoccupied with helping others that she overlooked
the needs of her own family. While Jennifer appeared
selfless to others, her family saw her as absorbed only in
what she wanted to do. Jennifer's selflessness was out of
balance.

One definition of selflessness is having no *undue*
concern for self. This thought implies that we do need

to be concerned about ourselves, just not excessively so. We do need to care about our health, our families, our responsibilities, and our appearance. To neglect ourselves to the extent that we forfeit our own well-being and the well-being of those around us ultimately negates our service.

The opposite of selflessness is selfishness, which is self-seeking, self-centered, self-indulgent, greedy, and uncharitable. The best example of someone who epitomizes self-centeredness is the mythological, handsome youth Narcissus. A pretty nymph, Echo, loved him, but because he considered his beauty to be unequaled, he spurned her affection. Heartbroken, Echo gradually faded away to a whisper. In order to teach Narcissus a lesson, the goddess Nemesis cursed him by making him fall in love with his own reflection. As he lay on the riverbank riveted by his countenance, he eventually wasted away.[18]

What a graphic description of someone who is "full of self." When anyone becomes totally focused on *self,* that person's soul seems to shrink.

> *If you are all wrapped up in yourself, you are overdressed.*[19]
> KATE HALVERSON

Becoming a Selfless Woman

There is a difference between feeling *compelled* to serve
and *choosing* to serve. Jennifer might have felt compelled
to serve out of her own need for recognition and attention. Amy Carmichael chose to serve because she was
self-assured and settled about her mission in life. She
willingly accepted the "sacrifice" of remaining single as
a necessary part of her serving others. It was her choice,
made from a position of strength. She was not a door-
mat to the children; instead she was a tower of strength
because she was secure in what she was doing. I think that
we must have a strong sense of *self* in order to be selfless.

> *We must have a strong sense of self
> in order to be selfless.*

I believe that Mary, the mother of Jesus, had
this strong sense of self. After being told by the angel
Gabriel that she was to have a baby who would be called
the Son of the Most High, she replied, "Yes, I see it all
now: I'm the Lord's maid, ready to serve. Let it be with
me just as you say."[20] Her response expresses the essence
of selflessness.

Knowing that she could trust God, Mary readily yielded her life to serve. Here was a young woman confident in who she was and therefore willing to wholeheartedly give of herself. I think that this is one reason God chose to use Mary; she had a clear understanding of herself, a fervent sense of selflessness, and the knowledge that in giving, one truly lives.

As we begin to realize the blessing of living selflessly, we become more sensitive to opportunities to serve. Donna's grandmother exemplified a selfless woman who saw a need and did something about it. Donna writes, "As a young girl, I never understood the relationship between my dad and my 'Aunt' Sally. I knew my dad's only sister had died when she was three. So who was Sally?

"I learned the answer when I was older and for the first time glimpsed the character of my grandmother, Violet Finlay. When my dad was a young boy during the Depression, a couple living in their neighborhood died in a murder-suicide. The couple's children were left with no living relatives—and no prospect except an orphanage and adoption into different families. My grandparents talked with a few Christian families on their street. No one had enough money in those days to care for

all of the children, but they realized that if each family
took in one child, the children would be able to grow up
around their siblings. So my grandmother raised Sally as
a daughter, while always helping her maintain her own
family identity. My grandmother also took in various
cousins and other relatives for months or years at a time.
Today, when couples often base their family planning on
the projected costs of raising a child, my grandmother's
life gives new meaning to the idea of selflessness."[21]

While Violet's selflessness was demonstrated by
caring for a young child, Jewell chose to act selflessly by
giving her daughter freedom to move overseas. When
Larisee told her mother, Jewell, that their family was
being transferred to England for three years, Larisee was
deeply touched by how her mother responded. Jewell, in
her late eighties at the time, knew that she would not be
able to travel overseas and that she would miss her grandson's graduation from high school. However, throughout the moving process, Jewell remained supportive
and upbeat. Once Larisee's family arrived in England,
Jewell sent care boxes of Jolly Ranchers and herbal tea.
She faithfully wrote letters and rejoiced in her daughter's
experiences in a foreign country. Not once in three years
did she ever make Larisee feel guilty.

Eight months after Larisee and her family returned to the States, Jewell died, but not until she saw all of the pictures and the video of her grandson's graduation.[22] What a gift Jewell gave her daughter. Her selflessness blessed the whole family and beautifully adorned this gracious, older woman.

Jewell was so different from Janice's mother, who could not accept her daughter's moving to another state. The mother's farewells consisted of "I can't believe you are leaving me." "You really know how to hurt your mother." "You better call me every day." "You need to be here for all the holidays."

The woman who is selfish is concerned only about how her life is affected by someone's decisions. She manipulates, feels sorry for herself, and makes others feel guilty for not meeting her needs. Selfishness builds walls, pushes people away, and is viewed as being most unattractive.

Mr. Darcy, one of the characters in Jane Austen's *Pride and Prejudice,* says, "I have been a selfish being all my life, in practice, though not in principle."[23] One of the reasons I like Jane Austen's writings so much is that her characters reflect my own heart. Certainly in principle I want to be selfless, but in practice I fail so often.

Frequently, I have thoughts like these: "I like having my own way." "I like it when other people pay attention to me." "Sometimes I serve, and no one says anything or notices what I have done." "It's not fair to give and not receive." I struggle with being selfless; I don't like being interrupted or giving up my agenda. I'm quite content-ed just to take care of my own life.

Since this is my nature, it is quite humorous that I gave birth to three children in three years. These babies invaded my space and my world. Not only did they invade, they took over. Suddenly, I had no choice; I could no longer just think about myself. Although those early years seem to be a blur, I was able to catch glimpses of my true self as I became lost in the needs of others.

On a wall in my home hangs a colorful painting of a unique, Picasso-like female creature who appears to be dancing. The woman's blouse has small yellow holes in it. In the margin of the artwork are these words: "She left pieces of her life everywhere she went. It's easier to feel the sunlight without them, she said."

I bought this artwork years ago to remind me to leave pieces of myself on my journey. It was through my children that I began to have small yellow holes in my soul that allowed me to begin to truly live.

I know it doesn't make sense, but it is in giving that we receive; it is in broadening our world to include others that we truly live; it is in being selfless that we become beautiful in the eyes of others and even beautiful and acceptable to ourselves.

When I take time to visit with a neighbor, talk with a friend who calls, drive a friend to a doctor's appointment, write a letter of encouragement, or volunteer to help those in need, I know that I have done what is right and good. Helping others is a way of helping myself to rise above my own small world and to feel the sunlight in my spirit.

> *It is in being selfless that we become beautiful.*

If I had to write a definition of selflessness, I think it would be this: willingly sacrificing one's self for the needs of others in order to truly live. This quality can be won only by making the hard decision to be concerned for others, by studying the lives of selfless women who have influenced our lives, and by understanding that giving to someone else ultimately blesses us in return. It is wise to practice selflessness, for it imparts an uncommon beauty and leaves the fragrance of a life well lived.

> *Selflessness is willingly sacrificing*
> *one's self for the needs of others*
> *in order to truly live.*

I am not an Amy Carmichael, serving overseas rescuing precious children. I am not an Anne Sullivan, investing in the life of a handicapped child. But perhaps I could become like Jewell and selflessly grant my children freedom. Or perhaps I could become like Della and willingly sacrifice something I value for someone I love. Or perhaps I could become like Lucille and in a moment of selflessness pack an extra lunch, and you and I could share a meal someday.

> *An ungiving person does not live; he breathes, he eats, he sleeps, he gratifies his needs, but only exists until he has discovered the cleverly interwoven secret of life, giving of oneself. True giving is done without the slightest trace of expecting to receive. Is it only in giving that we ever receive? Perhaps in giving of oneself there is enough taken away to have room to receive.*[24]
>
> ALICE R. PRATT

Questions for Reflection and Discussion

1. How would you define a selfless woman?

2. How does our culture view selflessness?

3. In your experience, who models or has modeled selflessness for you?

4. In what ways do other people consider you to be a selfless woman?

5. In what ways would you like to become a selfless woman?

6. What steps can you take to nurture a healthy selflessness in your life?

CHAPTER 5 *Graciousness*

*Small kindnesses, small courtesies,
small considerations, habitually
practiced in our social intercourse,
give a greater charm to the
character than the display of great
talents and accomplishments.*[1]

MARY ANN KELTY

Darla greeted me at the airport with a smile and a
hug. In the car she had a cold bottle of water waiting
for me. When we arrived at her home, she took me to
her guest room to unpack and get comfortable. She
had placed fresh flowers on the table, magazines in
a basket, and chocolates by the bed. Although I was
tired from my trip, I was refreshed by my friend's
gracious hospitality. These were all small courtesies

and considerations, but, indeed, I thought my hostess was most charming.

Graciousness is characterized by kindness, warm courtesy, unaffected politeness, and generosity of spirit. This generosity of spirit encompasses mercy and pardon. Gracious women are dignified, compassionate, pleasant, and hospitable. Their gracious personality is natural, spontaneous, and charming.

While traveling through the Dallas–Fort Worth Airport, I boarded the tram for the A and C concourse. I overheard a conversation between two women standing near me. One of them was obviously a newcomer to our country, and in broken English she asked the other woman where she would need to get off for the B concourse. Realizing that the visitor had gotten on the wrong tram, the American woman smiled reassuringly and told her that she would personally take her to her gate. Even though I knew that this would be out of the way for this most helpful woman, I could see that she didn't think twice. She instantly became a gracious ambassador.

This willing diplomat selflessly decided to escort this woman, but she was also gracious in the process. As I thought about her, I wondered if I should view her as being selfless or gracious. These two qualities are closely related, and together they bestow an exquisite beauty. But I think that there is a distinct difference between the two; each quality is unique in its own right.

As we read in the previous chapter, a selfless woman is beautiful because she doesn't focus on

Main Entry: gra-cious-ness
Pronunciation: 'grâ-shəs-nəs
a: quality of being kind and courteous **b:** tact and delicacy **c:** charm, good taste, generosity of spirit

herself; she has no pretense. A measure of her selflessness is in her serving and giving to others. On the other hand, while a gracious woman focuses on others, her graciousness is measured more by her kindnesses, her mercy, and her genial "air."

Years ago my path crossed an incredibly selfless woman. Her life had been spent in the service of others, and her altruistic nature did indeed make her attractive. But she was not necessarily warm and charming. She was pleasant and patiently answered all my questions, but she remained very distant and aloof, asking very few questions of me or anyone else. I left my meeting with her challenged by the selflessness she demonstrated in her years of service, but I would hesitate to describe her as gracious.

When I asked my friend Claire to describe the most gracious woman she knew, she immediately told me about Stephanie. "Stephanie is always glad to see you. If you visit her home, she gives you a big hug and says, 'Please come in and make yourself comfortable.' She instantly makes you feel special by being warm, affirming, and attentive to your needs. Most people want to talk about themselves, but Stephanie asks questions and is an excellent listener. She wants to know about you and your family. After a first meeting, she remembers that you drink tea instead of coffee."

> *The fragrance always stays in the hand that gives the rose.*[2]
> HADA BEJAR

Her Graciousness Blessed Others

These same attributes of graciousness were also found in Bobbi Olson, the wife of the University of Arizona basketball coach, Lute Olson. I regret that I never had the opportunity to meet her, but I felt I got to know her by reading the letters written in her honor after ovarian cancer took her life.

Because Bobbi's husband is an excellent coach and has won a national title, she was somewhat of a celebrity here in Tucson. But it was not just the basketball community who paid her tribute. It was the deli manager at the grocery store who said, "She was so pleasant, sweet and courageous, not to mention gorgeous. The day after every ball game Bobbi would visit our bakery-deli and buy a particular sweet pastry for Lute, the love of her life. She did this regardless of whether the team had won or lost."[3]

It was the workmen who wallpapered and painted her home: "When we were finishing the job, she asked us if we would like to go see a game. 'Well, sure,' we both said. It was the opening of the NCAA tournament hosted here in Tucson. She told us there would be tickets at the will-call window. Well, it was game day, and we went to find our seats. As we kept going down toward the court and got near the Wildcat bench, she turned and saw us and waved us to our seats right next to her! Wow, how could you ask for more?"

An eighteen-year-old wrote, "I met Bobbi only once, at a UA basketball banquet a couple of years ago. But she has acted as if we were lifelong buddies. . . . [When she died, it was] as if we all lost our favorite aunt."

At her memorial service, many of the players shared their love and respect for her. Former player

Matt Muehlebach commented, "Every player felt they were Bobbi's favorite. She seemed to know when to comfort us and when it was the right time to talk to us. She's called the team mom, but it was more than that; she was a great friend." Jason Terry said, "When I had my little girl, she'd always come up to her and talk to her. She always made it a point to do that, and she didn't have to, but that was just her. She loved everybody." A. J. Bramlett observed, "She made us feel like we were one of her own kids. She brought that family atmosphere to the team."

One of Lute Olson's recruiting tactics was to bring the new recruits to his home for one of Bobbi's pancake breakfasts. Corey Williams swore they were the best he'd ever tasted.

After Bobbi died, one of the newspaper headlines read, "Bobbi Olson's Living Legacy: Loyalty, Laughter and Love."[4] Truly, these words are a testimony to Bobbi's graciousness. Her life was full of small kindnesses, small courtesies, and small considerations that made her beautiful and charming to all who knew her.

Love is essentially the gift of oneself to another.[5]

MICHEL QUOIST

Her Graciousness Transformed a Role

Warm hospitality seems to be a natural expression of a gracious spirit. Bobbi entertained young basketball players with homemade pancakes. Darla and Stephanie are always ready to offer simple refreshments and comfortable surroundings to their guests. As I looked for a historical figure who became a role model for hospitality, my search led me to Dolley Madison.

What a delightful woman! She was the wife of James Madison, the fourth president of the United States. Dolley is known as the woman "who turned the new nation's capital at Washington, D.C., from a dull swamp into a high-society social scene. . . . Dolley created the role of First Lady as social hostess and trend-setter, furnishing the president's quarters for the first time and hosting weekly parties of politicians and citizens."[6]

Dolley is described as having a sparkling personality, an inviting manner, and a kind heart. Anyone would feel welcome at her gatherings. She cordially received hostile statesmen, difficult envoys, warrior chiefs, and flustered youngsters. Often her gracious tact enabled her to create calmness out of a tense political atmosphere. Part of her ability was due to her charm and part to her political astuteness.

She truly enjoyed entertaining and was noted for her surprise delicacies. Her Wednesday evening receptions were popular with politicians, diplomats, and the citizenry. During the War of 1812, the White House was destroyed by fire, so the Madisons moved to the Octagon House. However, this change did not deter Dolley from entertaining. Margaret Bayard Smith, chronicler of early Washington social life, wrote, "She looked a Queen. . . . It would be *absolutely impossible* for any one to behave with more perfect propriety than she did."[7]

Gracious women are generous with their time, their possessions, and their lives. Dolley is a good example of someone with a generous spirit. What I appreciate about her is that she *enjoyed* being gracious to others. True graciousness does bring joy to the one being gracious.

> *Grace was in all her steps, heav'n in her eye,*
> *In every gesture dignity and love.*[8]

JOHN MILTON

Her Graciousness Nourished a Leader

In the Bible we find another woman who fits this description of graciousness. Lydia lived during the first century in eastern Macedonia, in an area known for its unique purple dye. She was a well-known and prosperous businesswoman who sold expensive purple cloth.[9] One day the apostle Paul and his companion Silas went to a riverbank to meet with a group of people who gathered for prayer. There they met Lydia. As Paul spoke about the resurrected Christ, Lydia opened her heart and responded. That day she was baptized as a believer in Jesus Christ.

What did Lydia do immediately after she was baptized? She invited, even urged, Paul and Silas to come and stay at her home. And they accepted.

Lydia not only opened her heart, but she also graciously opened her home. She innately responded by being generous and hospitable.

I can only imagine the joy Lydia experienced during the time Paul and Silas stayed with her. Like Priscilla, about whom we read in the passion chapter, Lydia and her household probably had precious times of conversation with Paul. Her graciousness not only nourished her guests but also nourished her and her family.

Years ago I remember driving behind cars that had this bumper sticker: "Do Random Acts of Kindness." The thought was "*You* be kind to other people." The surprising truth about being kind and thoughtful to others is that not only does your kindness bless others, but you are blessed as well. One of King Solomon's proverbs confirms this idea: "Your own soul is nourished when you are kind."[10]

Somehow I think that if I do all the giving, then I'm left depleted. But that is not true. Whenever I take the time to be considerate, I realize that my soul has been nourished.

Whenever I take the time to be considerate, I realize that my soul has been nourished.

During a particularly busy time in my life, I felt prompted to invite a friend for lunch because I had heard that she was struggling with some family issues. I invited her rather reluctantly, but by the time she left, *I* was encouraged. Grace does that. Grace repays.

One evening my husband and I were eating in a

local restaurant when our server told us that a couple who wanted to remain anonymous had paid for our meal. We were surprised and looked around for someone we might know, but we didn't recognize anyone. Here were people who did what the bumper sticker exhorted them to do. Although their kindness was not random, it certainly had not been planned. The result of their spontaneous kindness was that all four of us were greatly blessed. Surely they left the restaurant with big smiles on their faces, as did we.

> *Often the nature of grace can be made plain only by describing its absence.*[11]

FLANNERY O'CONNOR

When Graciousness Is Absent

I was not in a particularly gracious mood when I invited my friend, but I chose to be hospitable nevertheless. However, sometimes people don't choose to override their feelings, and their lack of graciousness becomes evident. Such was Peninnah, a woman we read about in the Old Testament.[12] I smile when I think of her name. It is such a pretentious one; it fits her perfectly.

Peninnah's marriage was a recipe for disaster. Her

husband, Elkanah, had two wives: Peninnah and Hannah.
If that didn't create enough problems, Elkanah paid more
attention to Hannah than he did to Peninnah, making
her jealous.

Peninnah took out her jealousy by cruelly mock-
ing Hannah, who was unable to become pregnant. The
Bible tells us, "So Peninnah would taunt Hannah and
make fun of her because the Lord had kept her from
having children. Year after year it was the same—Peninnah would taunt Hannah as they went to the Taberna-
cle. Each time, Hannah would be reduced to tears and
would not even eat."[13]

Flannery O'Connor is right—the nature of grace
can be made plain by describing its absence, and Peninnah plainly exemplifies the absence of grace. Her
whole personality was devoid of warmth, kindness, and
compassion. She would never win "Mrs. Personality"
in a pageant! In fact the dictionary defines *graceless* as
devoid of attractive qualities.

> *The test of being a gracious woman*
> *is how we respond when the*
> *unexpected happens.*

I observed that kind of gracelessness recently at a charity luncheon. A woman who had arranged to have her friends sit with her arrived at her table to find three women whom she did not know sitting in her friends' seats. The situation was the result of a mix-up, of course, but instead of handling the situation with care and sensitivity, the woman made a big deal about the mistake and embarrassed the three women who had been told to sit there. The people sitting near that table were also embarrassed by the woman's lack of tact and grace.

Now, it is not wrong to want to correct an oversight, but the test of being a gracious woman is how we respond when the unexpected happens. Even in the awkwardness of a misunderstanding, we can still be courteous, kind, and helpful. This is the mark of a gracious woman.

> *Life appears to me too short to be spent in nursing animosity or registering wrongs.*[14]
>
> CHARLOTTE BRONTË

Her Graciousness Restored a Relationship

It is not easy to forgive or to be gracious, especially when we have been wronged, but circumstances do not dictate a gracious woman's response. In Shakespeare's play *King Lear* we meet Cordelia, a strong young woman who chose to grant grace at a great cost.

Old and vain, King Lear foolishly decided to divide his kingdom among his three daughters. He determined to make the divisions based on his assessment of each daughter's profession of her love for him. The two oldest daughters, Goneril and Regan, hypocritically declared their love for him by flattering him. Cordelia heard the falseness of their words and decided that, although she sincerely loved her father, she would not flatter him in order to be in his good graces or to inherit property.

Cordelia mused, "Then poor Cordelia! And yet not so, since I am sure my love's more ponderous than my tongue."[15] Essentially she thought, *I love my father dearly. My love is bigger than words, and he should know that.* As a result of her integrity and honesty, the king disinherited Cordelia and banished her from the kingdom. Lear's older daughters soon denied him all the trappings of kingship, and within a short period of time, Lear found himself homeless, daughterless, and powerless.

Later, when Cordelia returned from France to

try to rescue her father, she found a broken man. Lear acknowledged his wrong: "I know you do not love me, for your sisters have, as I do remember, done me wrong. You have some cause; they have not." Cordelia graciously responded, "No cause, no cause."[16]

What touches me is Cordelia's gracious embrace of her father in light of his mistreatment of her. Here was a gracious woman, willing to *for*give and *to* give love, regardless of what happened in the past. Life to her was too short to be spent in registering wrongs.

> *Forgiveness is the fragrance that the flower leaves on the heel of the one who crushed it.*[17]
>
> MARK TWAIN

Becoming a Gracious Woman

Cordelia did not dwell on what happened to her. She knew that holding on to a wrong will never make it right. A gracious woman is not only kind, hospitable, and courteous, but because of the grace that abides deeply within her, she is also able to be merciful and to offer forgiveness when she is hurt. A gracious woman is a grace giver, even to those who seem not to deserve it.

Some of the key synonyms for *grace* are forgiveness, mercy, reprieve, moral strength, and goodness. I'm not sure that someone who is unwilling to forgive can ever be truly gracious; the bitterness that results from withholding grace ultimately betrays our attempts to be gracious. Bitterness that is buried still flickers and rises up to manifest itself in ways that are hurtful to us and to others.

> *A gracious woman is a grace giver,*
> *even to those who seem not*
> *to deserve it.*

Bitterness makes us hard, unhappy, and unattractive. It was not long after meeting Gina that I realized that she had a hard and cold "air." She had been betrayed by a good friend and was not willing to talk with her or even to consider reconciliation, although the friend had made several attempts to reconcile. Gina seemed to enjoy nursing her hurt and went to great lengths to avoid this former friend and to let people know what had happened. She narrowed her circle of friends to only those who agreed with her and rejected anyone who had anything to do with her "enemy." Gina didn't realize it, but her ungraciousness was making her bitter, unhappy, and unattractive.

My good friend Jan enjoys talking about Lillian, her ninety-nine-year-old acquaintance whose pleasant face is softly wrinkled from smiling so much. Lillian's gracious spirit, though, is not the result of an easy, comfortable life. She has experienced, in her words, "family feuds and several broken relationships." Jan asked Lillian one time how she had lived so long and done so well, and Lillian's profound reply was, "I just refused to be offended."

I think that what is involved in refusing to be offended is the desire to forgive and to release others when we've been harmed. It is deciding that forgiveness is always the best choice. Paula Rinehart writes, "Being unable or unwilling to forgive means that you remain emotionally under the control of the person who wronged you. Which is a bit ironic, don't you think? Here you are, desperately wanting to break free from the pain of it all, but unforgiveness is like Brer Rabbit and the Tar Baby—everything under the sun sticks to it. We *ourselves* are stuck to it. A harbored wrong can control a life."[18] Gina is living proof that bitterness is a hard taskmaster who keeps us tied to the very person

we don't want to be around. In reality, being gracious is
the best choice for *us*. In forgiving, we nourish our own
soul, and we are then free to be gracious to all we meet.

In forgiving, we nourish our own soul,
and we are then free to be gracious
to all we meet.

I am reminded of two sisters, Doris and Fran,
who married two brothers, George and Greg. Over
the course of time, due to some extenuating circumstances, George publicly humiliated his brother. He
severed all ties, and vowed that he and Doris would
never speak to Greg or Fran again. Fran, particularly, was devastated. She was humiliated along with
her husband, and she lost her sister in the process.
Through the years, though, Fran would send letters
and gifts to Doris, but Doris would return them. Fran
continued to extend grace to her sister by communi-
cating through others, "Anytime you want to see me,
I'm available."

Eventually, George died, and Doris sent a message
to her sister saying, "I will come see you, but we will

not talk about what happened." Fran graciously accepted her terms, and this was the beginning of the resto-
ration of their relationship. Because Fran forgave
her sister and welcomed her back into her life, they
were able, over a period of time, to talk about what
happened and be reconciled. But if Fran had responded as Gina did by drawing a hard line and becoming
bitter, then she and her sister would never have been
able to be friends again. Fran believed that life was
too short to nurse animosity, and I believe that Doris
could not help but smell the fragrance of her sister's
forgiveness.

Fran and Doris learned the truth of what Joan
Lunden said: "Holding on to anger, resentment, and
hurt only gives you tense muscles, a headache and a
sore jaw from clenching your teeth. Forgiveness gives
you back the laughter and the lightness in your life."[19]
Forgiveness allowed the two sisters to regain their
friendship, their laughter—and their lives.

Being gracious does not mean that we don't experience pain when we've been wounded, but it does
mean that we are willing to deal with the pain and to
come out on the side of grace. A survivor of sexual
abuse wrote, "I do not believe that my family deserves

forgiveness, but that is not the point. I longed to be free from the bitterness and rage that were destroying me. Slowly, I began to open myself up to the possibility of forgiveness, and my life began to change. God softened my heart and filled me with love. It was like opening the windows on a beautiful spring day. I believe that forgiveness is part of the healing process and is itself a process."[20]

> *Being gracious means that we*
> *are willing to deal with the pain and*
> *to come out on the side of grace.*

What can we say? A gracious woman almost seems to be the ideal woman, and it is overwhelming to think that we, too, can measure up to all that graciousness entails. How can we begin to acquire a gracious spirit? I think that we can begin by practicing random acts of kindness. Perhaps we can start by being kind to the person at the checkout counter in the grocery store. We can hold open a door for someone. We can invite a neighbor over for coffee. We can take a friend to lunch. We can send birthday cards. We can experience what it is like to open the windows on a beautiful spring day by releasing our bitterness and forgiving those who have hurt us.

We can set our hearts to become women whose grace is evident in all our steps, "in every gesture dignity and love." We will not be perfect, but we will have a special, gracious, fragrant, uncommon beauty because of our small kindnesses, small courtesies, small considerations, and great compassion.

> *The quality of mercy is not strain'd;*
> *It droppeth as the gentle rain from heaven*
> *Upon the place beneath: it is twice bless'd;*
> *It blesseth him that gives and him that takes.*[21]

WILLIAM SHAKESPEARE

Questions for Reflection and Discussion

1. How would you describe a gracious woman?

2. How does our culture view grace and graciousness?

3. In your experience, who models or has modeled graciousness for you?

4. In what ways do other people consider you to be gracious?

5. In what ways would you like to become a gracious woman?

6. What steps can you take to nurture graciousness in your life?

CHAPTER 6 *Contentment*

Cheerfulness and contentment are great beautifiers, and are famous preservers of youthful looks, you may depend upon it.[1]

CHARLES DICKENS

My friend Laura is a single mom whose husband left her more than twenty years ago. With determination and lots of prayer, she has raised three boys on her own and now has adult sons of whom she is most proud. She has retired from nursing and is living on a fixed income in a nice mobile-home park. She has not let pain and rejection keep her from living a fulfilled life.

When I was with Laura recently, I told her that I was writing a chapter about contentment and that I was looking for stories of contented women. She turned to me and said softly, "Cynthia, I am contented." I was humbled by her response. I knew that what she said was true. Every time I have been with her, she has been positive and at peace. Although she has been deeply hurt and has experienced hard times, she has accepted her situation and chosen contentment over disillusionment.

The classic definition of contentment is to be pleased with our situation to the point that we don't want any change or improvement. That is indeed a wonderful place to be, but given the realities of life, we rarely get to stay in circumstances that are ideal. Laura was pleased with her life until her husband announced that he was leaving. Her circumstances drastically changed, and she needed to redefine what it meant to be contented.

The definition I like is one I heard years ago. It characterizes contentment as being satisfied—satisfied not because something is in sufficient supply, but satisfied with whatever is available. This is what Laura did. She realized that it was necessary to be satisfied with what was available. And what was available was a life without a husband and without a father for her children. She didn't know what the future would hold, but she knew that for the moment, she could do nothing to change her circumstances. Laura decided to make the best of her situation and live as fully as possible. She chose to be grateful for what she had—and not to be discontented over what she did not have.

It is critical that in our quest for contentment, we don't miss the opportunity of being contented along the way. We need to live in the present, as writer Annie Dillard reminds us, "Spend the afternoon. You can't take it with you."[2] We also need to realize that contentment springs from within us. Martha Washington realized that truth. She wrote, "The greater part of our happiness or misery depends on our dispositions and not our circumstances."[3] Contentment is a choice, a learned attitude. The apostle Paul reminds us, "Not that I was ever in need, for I have learned how to be content with whatever I have."[4]

Main Entry: con-tent-ment
Pronunciation: kən-'tənt-mənt
a: the state or quality of being contented
b: satisfaction with one's situation

> *Contentment is a choice,*
> *a learned attitude.*

If the present is not to our liking and it cannot be readily changed, then we should set our hearts,

our dispositions, to learn contentment in spite of
our circumstances. Learning to be contented involves
choosing to accept the circumstances we are in and
doing all that we can to make the best of them. I've
heard it said, "You play with the hand you are dealt."
I would revise it in this way: "Play with the hand you
are dealt, and enjoy the game as much as possible."

No one has played the hand she was dealt better
than my very dear friend Jan, who had polio as a young
girl. When I first met Jan, she had braces on her legs
and used hand crutches to walk. Now this devastating
disease has come back, and she is confined to a wheelchair and a motor scooter. She lives with pain and with
the reality that her body will continue to weaken. But
Jan has never been one to stay home and feel sorry for
herself. She has more friends than anyone I know, and
she frequently flies or drives to visit them.

She is now retired from teaching and has stayed
very active in the national high school organization
Young Life. She is an amazing woman who lives a full
life in spite of her disability. She has a great sense of
humor and is fun to be around. Amazed that Jan travels so much, her older sister teased her, "Jan, don't
you know that you are single and handicapped?" Jan

cannot change the fact that she has polio, but she has continually chosen contentment even as her circumstances change.

Mary Gracianette was also willing to play with the hand she was given. Mary ran the kitchen for the Deckbar and Grille outside of New Orleans, and when Hurricane Katrina hit that area, she decided to stay and help anyone seeking shelter and food. Mary ran a "makeshift hospice-hostel-soup kitchen" for weeks. When her supplies ran out, she relied on donations to feed those in need. Mary was not only gracious and selfless, but she was also an example of someone who was grateful to live and serve with whatever was available.[5]

Contentment that is based on the reality that nothing can be changed to make our circumstances more suitable is the contentment that becomes a great beautifier and preserver of youthful looks. I know that Jan's youthful looks have been preserved, and I suspect Mary's have too.

> *No life is so hard that you can't make it easier by the way you take it.*[6]

ELLEN GLASGOW

Contentment in Making the Most of So Little

One of the most contented women I've ever met is
Jesse Goddard. My husband and I met Jesse and her
husband, Ceph, in 1960, while Jack was testing cattle
for brucellosis in North Dakota. When Jack and I
went out to their ranch, they graciously invited us
to dinner at their log cabin. I was amazed to watch
Jesse prepare a delicious dinner over her woodstove,
all with water she had drawn by hand. She served us
steak, fresh vegetables, and homemade bread. After
the main course, she took her iron skillet and made
crêpes suzette. I'm from Houston, and I had never
had them in my life. Here I was in the middle of
nowhere, in a log cabin with a dirt floor, eating crêpes
suzette. To top off the elegant experience, Jesse gave
us a finger bowl with a small lemon in it to wash our
hands.

I came away with a sense of Jesse's inner contentment because her "wants" were few. Not having a crêpe
pan or running water didn't keep Jesse from entertaining in style. She modeled being contented with
what was at hand.

Jesse lived in somewhat the same conditions that the pioneer women lived. As I thought about women who had to learn to be contented with what was available, my first thoughts were of the brave women who lived in harsh conditions with no amenities. Most of us are familiar with the *Little House on the Prairie* books, in which Laura Ingalls Wilder wrote about her family's adventures as they homesteaded in the Dakota Territory. Laura writes fondly about her mother, Caroline Ingalls, who responded with grace and fortitude to pioneer life and who exemplified being contented with what was available. At their first settlement, Caroline lived for months with a limited supply of cornmeal. She had no milk, butter, or vegetables. And she patiently waited for her husband to build a cabin and dig a well. Since her wants were very basic and few, she was most pleased with a rocking chair that Pa made for her. After her husband built their log cabin home, he commented, "I wish we had glass for the windows." Caroline replied, "We don't need glass, Charles."[7]

> *Contentment comes not so much from great wealth*
> *as from few wants.*[8]
>
> EPICTETUS

Contentment Lost

Jesse's and Caroline's surroundings were not what many of us would consider as ideal, but even if our circumstances were perfect, would we still be contented? Our answer is found in the Garden of Eden as we observe Eve, a woman who had everything she needed and yet wanted more. In a way, we are all daughters of Eve, and I guess that we are prone to question if what we have is really enough. We believe that we might be missing out on something, and we find ourselves driven and pulled to unwisely reach out and taste whatever is marketed as the special "fruit" that will make us happy or better or more complete. Eve and Adam paid an incredibly high price for their discontentment. And so will we, until at some point we learn that the secret of contentment is to be grateful for and aware of how much we already have.

The secret of contentment is to be grateful for and aware of how much we already have.

Sharon approached me after a meeting and asked if she could talk to me about how to help her neigh-

bor Betsy. From the time Betsy moved into the neighborhood, she was negative. She told Sharon that she
wasn't pleased with her house, she didn't like the nearby stores, and she definitely didn't like the climate.
Sharon even hosted an informal coffee so that Betsy
could meet some other women. But after a year, Betsy
was still unhappy, and her negativity had driven away
any potential new friends. Needless to say, Betsy's
discontentedness was not helping to preserve her
youthful looks.

And what did Betsy have to be grateful and
contented about? A good husband, healthy children,
a nice home, and money for clothing and food. But
instead of choosing contentment, she chose to be
ungrateful and miserable. What a waste of time! If only
she had been willing to accept the reality that this was
where she was to live for the present and that since she
couldn't readily change her circumstances, her best
option was to be satisfied with what was available.

In my own way, I can identify with Betsy's feelings
about her house. Early in our marriage, my husband
bought a veterinary practice in a small, central Texas
town. Included in the purchase was a sixty-year-old
duplex that needed a lot of tender loving care to make

it a home. But since we planned to live in this house only until our finances were stable enough to buy a nicer home, we spent as little money as possible to make it livable.

At that time we were a family of five, and we lived in both sides of the duplex. That meant I had to use one of the kitchens as a bedroom for our three-year-old. (Have you ever tried to decorate a kitchen as a bedroom?) As my husband and I made friends, they graciously invited us to their lovely, one-kitchen homes, but I was reluctant to invite anyone to our house. When I compared my home with everyone else's, I was discontented.

However, in the midst of my situation, I was able to recall the words that I heard my grandmother say many times, "Well, if that's the way it has to be, then we'll make the best of it." So I settled into the old duplex, made the best of it, and began learning the hard and humbling lesson of being satisfied with what is available.

Contentment is not the fulfillment of what you want, but the realization of how much you already have.

ANONYMOUS

Contentment in the Midst of Disappointment

Jane Bennet, the likable oldest sister in *Pride and Prejudice*, has always impressed me with her cheerfulness and contentment. She is friendly, optimistic, and good-natured. Elizabeth, her sister and best friend, tells Jane, "You never see a fault in anybody. . . . You are too good!"

Even when Jane's suitor, Mr. Bingley, leaves abruptly and moves back to London, she chooses to accept the situation with grace and a positive attitude. When Jane and Elizabeth talk, Elizabeth suggests that it was Mr. Bingley's sisters who persuaded him to leave. Jane responds, "Do not distress me by the idea. I am not ashamed of having been mistaken—or, at least, it is slight, it is nothing in comparison of what I should feel in thinking ill of him or his sisters. Let me take it in the best light, in the light in which it may be understood."[9] This was Jane's way—to make the most of whatever happened. Is not this contentment: accepting whatever dark circumstances we encounter and at least attempting to place them in the best light?

Jane's willingness to reconcile herself to her situation enabled her to go on with her life even though it was not what she wanted. But eventually the good Mr. Bingley returns and proposes. Jane's patience is rewarded, and she exclaims, "I am certainly the most fortunate creature that ever existed! . . . Oh! Lizzy, why am I thus singled from my family, and blessed above them all! If I could but see *you* as happy! If there *were* but such another man for you!"

Elizabeth replied, "If you were to give me forty such men, I never could be so happy as you. Till I have your disposition, your goodness, I never can have your happiness."[10] Elizabeth's acknowledgment of Jane's sweet disposition authenticates Jane's intrinsic contentment. Of the five Bennet sisters, Jane was known as the most beautiful; I wonder if her cheerfulness and contentment were her great beautifiers? I think that Dickens would say yes.

> *Contentment is being able to enjoy the scenery when*
> *you are taking a detour.*[11]
>
> GERALD R. PAYNE

Contentment in the Face of Loss

I think we all are drawn to love stories like Cinderella, where the heroine is poor and has little hope of love, but through impossible circumstances she meets Prince Charming, and they live happily ever after. That is also the story of Ruth, whose life is described in the Bible.[12]

Ruth's story begins with a famine. Because of a severe food shortage in the town of Bethlehem, a woman named Naomi and her family moved to Moab (part of present-day Jordan). While there, Naomi's husband died, and her two sons married Moabite women, Ruth and Orpah. However, about ten years later, both of Naomi's sons died as well, leaving the three women alone. In that culture, widows were cared for by the males of the family, and since Naomi had no other male family members in Moab, she decided to return home to Bethlehem.

Naomi encouraged Ruth and Orpah to stay in their own country so that they could remarry. Orpah chose to stay in Moab, but Ruth insisted on accompanying her mother-in-law to Bethlehem. Here is one of the first indications of Ruth's desire to be satisfied with what she had. She was given the opportunity to seek contentment in the security of her own country, family, and friends, yet she chose to stay with her mother-in-law. Ruth's words to Naomi are often repeated at weddings: "Wherever you go, I will go; wherever you live, I will live. Your people will be my people, and your God will be my God."[13] These are great declarations of satisfaction with the life she was to lead.

When Ruth and Naomi arrived in Bethlehem, Ruth began to glean—one of the lowliest tasks in that culture. Daily she followed the reapers in the barley fields and gathered fragments of grain left behind for the poor. The Bible makes no mention that Ruth felt sorry for herself or that she complained about what she had to do. She worked hard, and the field hands were impressed by her attitude.

One day Ruth gleaned in the field of Boaz, a wealthy and noble landowner. He noticed her—was it her beauty?—and took a special interest in her situation. Boaz had heard about Ruth's love and kindness toward her mother-in-law, and he invited her to stay in his fields, where he could protect her. Boaz also instructed his workers to drop extra food for Ruth to gather.

When Ruth told her mother-in-law about her conversation with Boaz, Naomi was excited. She realized that Boaz was a close relative, one of their family's "kinsman-redeemers." This is important because Ruth's husband had died without giving her a child, and in that culture, it was the responsibility of a close relative—of the kinsman-redeemer—to marry her and provide an heir for her deceased husband.

Naomi instructed Ruth to go that night to Boaz's threshing floor and to lie at his feet. Ruth obeyed her mother-in-law, and when Boaz awakened, she asked for his protection, which was essentially a legal call on him to fulfill the duty of the closest relative: to purchase Naomi's land in Bethlehem and to marry Ruth so that she could produce an heir. Boaz responded to Ruth's request with these warm words of blessing: "May you be blessed of the Lord, my daughter. You have shown your last kindness to be better than the first by not going after young men, whether poor or rich. Now, my daughter, do not fear. I will do for you whatever you ask, for all my people in the city know that you are a woman of excellence."[14]

Boaz was grateful and pleased by Ruth's request, but he could not act immediately because he was not the *closest* relative. He was obligated first to give a closer relative the first opportunity to redeem Ruth.

Uncertain of what would happen, Boaz went to the town gate, where he approached the other relative and told him about his opportunity to redeem Naomi's family's land. The man said, "All right, I'll redeem it."

But when Boaz told him that if he redeemed the land, he would also have to marry Ruth, the other relative changed his mind: "Then I can't redeem it because this might endanger my own estate. You redeem the land; I cannot do it."

In the end, Ruth married Boaz, and they lived happily ever after. They even became great-grandparents to the future King David.

No one seems to exemplify contentment as much as Ruth. And perhaps it is that great beautifier—content-ment—that compels everyone who writes about her to depict her as a beauty. Although we have no picture of Ruth, Irving Fineman describes her as a woman "whose radiant beauty of face and form neither the shadows nor the sad state of her raiment could obscure."[15]

The story of Ruth is one of my favorites. The part I like best is when Boaz said that everyone who knew Ruth appreciated her virtuous, noble, and excellent character. But how could Ruth possibly be known for her noble character? We would expect her to be known as "poor widow Ruth" or as a "woman of hopelessness," certainly not as a "woman of excellence," for she had absolutely nothing going for her. She was a widow living in a foreign country, helping a grieving mother-in-law by doing the most menial work possible. And Ruth did all this with no hope that anything would ever change. But isn't this the essence of contentment—living life with an excellent character, whatever our circumstances? Ruth took the detour offered her, but she enjoyed the scenery along the way. No wonder she is portrayed as beautiful; she chose contentment.

> *Contentment is living life*
> *with an excellent character,*
> *whatever our circumstances.*

Becoming a Woman of Contentment

So how do we become women of excellence, women who choose contentment? The contentment that is a great beautifier conveys an inner sense of satisfaction with who we are and what we have. To gain contentment, we must be willing to give up trying to prove ourselves or wanting more in order to be accepted.

I find that one of the greatest threats to my sense of contentment is the temptation to compare myself with others. I notice those who have nicer homes, more friends, or more ability than I have. I become like Eve—

wanting more than what I have, even though what I have is more than enough.

Do you ever feel that way too? The women whose stories we have looked at in this chapter inspire me. They faced losses, obstacles, and handicaps, yet they chose to accept what was available. When I think about the lives of many women around the world, I am sobered and convicted. If I have food in my refrigerator, if I am dressed and have shoes, if I have a bed and a roof above my head, I am better off than 75 percent of people in this world.[16] When I live in such abundance, I have no need to ever complain. And since I have so much to be thankful for, I have no need to seek after glory for myself.

I am old enough to say that life is lived all too quickly. The Bible says, "You're nothing but a wisp of fog, catching a brief bit of sun before disappearing."[17] Life on earth is short.[18] Since this is true, then it seems that learning contentment should be a high priority. I don't want to become an unattractive old woman who has rarely been satisfied and whose disposition and face reflect discontentedness. How sad to go through life as a disgruntled, unhappy, unlovely woman. As I grow older, I want to be like Verda.

Verda was the mother-in-law of my special friend Debby. One of Verda's favorite phrases was, "I'm just so blessed." Whenever she had an ache or pain, she would mention it but then immediately say, "But I don't have anything to complain about." When Debby and the rest of the family moved Verda out of her spacious apartment of thirty-five years into a one-room apartment in an assisted-living home, Verda's response was, "Why, I just have everything I need—my favorite table, my bed, and my pictures. I don't miss anything." People in the home described Verda as the bright spot in their day. She had a sweet, cheerful smile for everyone.

After Verda died, her family found among her belongings numerous articles and quotations about contentment and a positive attitude. Verda had collected—and practiced—the truth about contentment, and everyone around her benefited from her choice.

We gain contentment by choosing to accept what cannot be changed and learning to be grateful and satisfied with what is available.

Contentment is a quality that can be learned mostly by being thankful for what we have in the present moment. It is choosing to be thankful for the scenery when we are forced to take a detour. If Laura, Jan, Jesse, Ruth, and Verda could decide to be contented, so can we. We gain contentment by choosing to accept what cannot be changed and learning to be grateful and satisfied with what is available. And what do we have to gain? A cheerful spirit, youthful good looks, and uncommon beauty. You can depend on it.

Happiness is the best facelift.[19]

JONI MITCHELL

Questions for Reflection and Discussion

1. How would you describe a contented woman?

2. How does our culture view contentment?

3. In your experience, who models or has modeled contentment for you?

4. In what ways do other people consider you to be a contented woman?

5. In what ways would you like to become a contented woman?

6. What steps can you take to nurture contentment in your life?

CHAPTER 7 *Courage*

I do not ask to walk smooth paths
nor bear an easy load.
I pray for strength and fortitude
to climb the rock strewn road.

Give me such courage and I can scale
the hardest peaks alone,
And transform every stumbling block
into a stepping stone.[1]

GAIL BROOK BURKET

When Dolley Madison was faced with imminent
danger, she chose to stand her ground with strength
and fortitude. It was 1812, and British troops
were advancing toward Washington with the goal
of destroying the city. President James Madison,
Dolley's husband, had been called away temporar-

ily, leaving her alone at the White House with only a
servant. As cannon fire struck nearby, Dolley filled
a wagon with Cabinet papers and the most valuable portable articles belonging to the White House.
She had no time or room to save any of her personal
property.

Here is what she wrote to her sister, Anna, as she
departed the White House: "Our kind friend, Mr.
Carroll, has come to hasten my departure, and in
a very bad humor with me, because I insist on waiting until the large picture of General Washington is
secured, and it requires to be unscrewed from the wall.
This process was found too tedious for these perilous moments; I have ordered the frame to be broken,
and the canvas taken out. It is done! And the precious
portrait placed in the hands of two gentlemen of New
York for safekeeping. And now, dear sister, I must
leave this house, or the retreating army will make me
a prisoner in it by filling up the road I am directed to
take. When I shall again write to you, or where I shall
be tomorrow, I cannot tell!"[2]

The landscape of history is more beautiful because
Dolley resolved to stay behind and save not only vital
state documents but also Gilbert Stuart's famous

portrait of George Washington. Dolley Madison became
a symbol of bravery because she was willing to face an
advancing army and "climb the rock strewn road."

Courage is not
typically regarded as a
great beautifier, but
an uncommon beauty
emerges in women who
confront danger and
hardship. A woman

Main Entry: cour-age
Pronunciation: 'kər-ij
a: mental or emotional strength to persevere
and withstand danger, fear, or difficulty
b: ability to hold one's own or keep up one's
morale when opposed or threatened **c**: spirit
and tenacity **d**: ability to endure adversity

who has been tested possesses an inner strength that
sets her apart and gives her a distinctive "air" that is,
indeed, attractive.

> *A woman who has been tested*
> *possesses an inner strength that*
> *sets her apart.*

When I think of courage, I think of women who
persevere through difficult and sometimes dangerous
circumstances. Courageous women stand firm when
their ideas or goals are threatened. They refuse to quit
when life gets hard. They are women who have spunk

and heart. Even when the world around them seems to crumble, courageous women rise to the occasion.

In a way, every woman who has ever lived has had to be courageous. So much of life requires us to gather our moral strength and be steadfast.

> *Courage is not the absence of fear, but rather the judgment that something else is more important than fear.*[3]

AMBROSE REDMOON

Courage in the Face of Danger

Having courage does not mean we will never feel afraid. Courage propels us to act in spite of our fear, not allowing the fear to dictate our behavior.

A striking example of this is a Chechnyan woman who overcame her fear because the life of her son was more important. One morning armed rebels demanded that her twenty-three-year-old son come out of the house. They intended to force him to become part of their army. As the militants were taking the son to their jeep, his mother blocked their path. She stood her ground and challenged the rebels, "You will have to kill me first." Apparently they were so stunned by her courage that they released her son.[4]

Molly Hays also gathered her moral strength and acted in spite of her fear. Molly's husband was an artilleryman in George Washington's army, and she insisted on accompanying her husband into battle. When people objected to her decision, she said, "I can help the soldiers when they are in trouble, and I can stand it as well as he." As the soldiers fought in the extreme heat, Molly not only dressed their wounds but also grabbed a bucket and carried water from a cool spring to the thirsty men. The soldiers began to call her "Molly Pitcher."

Later that day Molly's husband was wounded and was no longer able to man the cannon. As the soldiers prepared to abandon the gun, Molly grabbed the rammer and began swabbing and reloading the cannon. She stayed at her post in the face of enemy fire and encouraged the others by saying, "Stand fast." Emboldened by her courage, the soldiers stood their ground and forced the British army to retreat. The next day she was taken to General George Washington, who told her, "You have made a brave stand. We will win our liberty if we all stand fast like you."[5]

Standing fast in the face of the enemy is what Harriet Tubman did all of her life. Born into slavery, the young Harriet was cruelly treated. When the twelve-year-old girl refused to tie up a slave who was trying to escape, the white slave boss hit her in the head, causing serious injury. At the age of twenty-five, she married a free African-American and later escaped to Canada via the Underground Railroad. Over a ten-year period, she made numerous trips back to the South to lead slaves to safety.

During those trips she evaded slave-catchers and bloodhounds, endured attacks and beatings, and courageously persevered in spite of a $40,000 reward offered by slaveholders for her capture, dead or alive. She went on to serve as a nurse and a spy during the war, and to work on behalf of former slaves in the South. As the first woman "conductor" on the Underground Railroad during the Civil War, she was responsible for rescuing three hundred slaves.[6]

When Juliana Dogbadzi, from the West African country of Ghana, was seven years old, her parents sent her to a shrine to become a slave for a fetish priest. The parents engaged in this religious and cultural practice, known as *Trokosi,* to atone for the alleged crimes of their relatives. For seventeen years Juliana cleaned the compound, worked in the priest's fields, and prepared meals for the priest. She herself was given little to eat, had very little clothing, and had no medical care. The priest also used her for sex. After a daring escape, Juliana, now twenty-six, travels the country speaking out against *Trokosi* and trying to win freedom for other slaves. She visits shrines and talks to the female slaves, telling them that they need to gather courage and escape their situation.[7] "What I do is dangerous, but I am prepared to die for a good cause."[8] Juliana's passion to rescue young girls from the life she knows all too well propels her to act in spite of her fear. Her courage makes her a beautiful woman.

> *A woman is like a tea bag. You never know how strong she is until she gets into hot water.*[9]
>
> ELEANOR ROOSEVELT

Courage That Confronts Evil

The 1958 classic film *The Inn of the Sixth Happiness,* starring Ingrid Bergman, is based on the true story of Gladys Aylward, a resolute young woman who worked as a maid in London but was convinced that she should become a missionary to China.[10] She went to a training school but was told that she would never be able to learn the language.

This did not stop Gladys. She saved her money and on her own undertook an arduous and dangerous trip to China to assist an older missionary. The two women opened the Inn of the Sixth Happiness, where they cared for travelers and told them Bible stories. Gladys eventually learned five different dialects of Chinese.

One day while traveling, Gladys found a beggar who was using a malnourished child to attract money. Moved by compassion, Gladys rescued the child and cared for her. She later took in an abandoned boy, and over the years her "family" grew to almost one hundred children. After the Japanese invaded China in 1937, Gladys fled with the children and began a perilous journey to safety. Fearful that the soldiers would find them, they trekked across mountains enduring hunger, cut and blistered feet, and little sleep. After several weeks, they finally reached a city that would take refugees. Gladys immediately collapsed and almost died. She was suffering from a severe fever of 105°, typhus, pneumonia, malnutrition, and exhaustion, but she had not lost her courage.[11]

Jehosheba, whose story is told in the Bible, was another courageous woman who saved the life of an

innocent child.[12] After King Ahaziah had been killed,
his evil mother, Athaliah, seized the throne and set out
to murder the remaining royal heirs. This meant that
she killed her own grandchildren.

Determined to foil the malevolent intentions of the
king's mother and preserve the royal lineage, Jehosheba,
the wife of the priest, took the king's infant son and hid
him from his grandmother's rage. The boy, Joash, was
raised in the Temple for six years.

When Joash was seven years old, the priest summoned his own courage and decided to bring Joash out
of hiding. Protecting the boy with armed guards and
surrounding him with the civil and military leaders of
the day, the priest anointed and crowned Joash king.
Had Jehosheba not summoned her moral courage and
rescued Joash, the royal line of Judah would have been
extinct. It was from this line that Jesus was born.

Times do not seem to change. Courage is still
needed to confront evil. As Monique Williams was driving home from the grocery store one day, she observed
a ten-year-old girl entering a car with a lone man at
the wheel. Monique felt that something was not right,
so she called out to the young girl, "You know him?"
When the girl indicated that she did not, Monique

drove her van in front of the car, effectively blocking it. Then she made sure that the girl got out.

The police arrested the man, and Williams received a civilian commendation and a plaque from the girl: "To my guardian angel, Monique Williams. I love you. Chiara Rufus."[13]

Indeed, each of these women, in her own way, was a guardian angel—to soldiers, children, slaves, or national treasures. They encountered danger and judged that freedom and justice were far more precious than their own fear or their own lives. These are truly courageous, beautiful women who will forever serve as role models for strength and bravery.

> I *wanted you see what real courage is, instead of getting the idea that courage is a man with a gun in his hand. It's when you know you're licked before you begin, but you begin anyway and you see it through no matter what.*[14]
>
> HARPER LEE

Courage for the Long Haul

Although courage is most frequently associated with confronting perilous circumstances, its expression cannot be limited only to adrenaline-charged moments.

There are countless brave women who demonstrate their courage by living day after day in the face of adversity.

Susan B. Anthony is renowned for waging an unceasing battle for women's rights. In 1869 she and Elizabeth Cady Stanton formed the National Women's Suffrage Association. For thirty long years, they endured attacks from both men and women, but they courageously persevered by laying a powerful groundwork for the next generation of women to win the right to vote in 1920.[15]

But it is an incident in 1872 that vividly demonstrates Susan B. Anthony's courage and tenacity. Susan and fourteen women went to the polls and insisted on voting. They cast their ballots, but a few days later Susan was arrested and brought before a judge for illegally entering a voting booth.

"How do you plead?" asked the judge.

"Guilty!" cried Susan. "Guilty of trying to uproot the slavery in which you men have placed us women. Guilty of trying to make you see that we mothers are as important to this country as are the men. Guilty of trying to lift the standard of womanhood, so that men may look with pride upon their wives' awareness of public affairs. . . . But not guilty of acting against the

Constitution of the United States, which says that no
person is to be deprived of equal right under the law."

The judge was taken aback but quietly said, "I am
forced to fine you one hundred dollars."

Susan replied, "I will not pay it! Mark my words,
the law will be changed!" And with that she left.

When the judge was asked if she needed to be
brought back, he answered, "No, let her go. I fear that
she is right and that the law will soon be changed."[16]
Although neither Susan nor Elizabeth was able to
experience the fruit of their hard-fought battle, they
were determined to "see it through no matter what."

This is what Vanessa continues to do on a daily
basis. Catherine wrote me about her good friend
Vanessa, who was engaged to be married. A few months
before the wedding, her fiancé had an accident that
left him a quadriplegic. Like Margaret, whom we met
in the integrity chapter, Vanessa could have walked
away from her fiancé, but she chose to marry Johnny
and to become his primary caregiver for the rest of
her life.

For more than twenty years she has single-handed-
ly cared for her husband. Johnny cannot be left alone.
He needs help dressing himself, feeding himself, and

using the bathroom. Vanessa also does all of the necessary maintenance for their home and yard.

Many of Vanessa's dreams died the day Johnny's body was broken, but some dreams have come true. A few years after the accident, Johnny graduated from college with honors. He now has a successful career managing databases for a medical services company. They have three lovely children. Through sheer hard work, Johnny and Vanessa have forged a nearly normal life. Catherine comments, "Their life is so normal that it's easy to almost forget about the wheelchair." Vanessa is the first to admit that it has not been easy, but then real courage is never easy.[17]

Janet Eckles's triumphant spirit is an inspiration to keep going despite seemingly insurmountable difficulty. She wrote to me, "A retinal disease robbed my sight and with it my motivation and sense of purpose. Clichés annoyed me, but this one nudged my soul: Attitude determines your altitude. I looked up, and in prayer, I sought wisdom. I began to walk with the white cane of determination. With the tools God provided, I set off to fulfill my desire to write. Using a voice synthesizer to operate my computer, I entered the new world of technology.

"Equipped with my new vision, I struggled through the process. And overcoming moments of frustration, impatience, and constant temptation to give up, I plunged forth. Once I memorized the numerous key commands needed for each application, I began to describe each episode in my life: the devastating loss of my sight, the pain of infidelity, and the anguish of losing my youngest son.

"With each line and paragraph, I satisfied the urge to shout from the mountaintops, 'You can turn adversity to opportunities and disabilities to abilities.' The years swept by, the chapters fit together, and the ending highlights details of triumph and victory. I titled my book *Trials of Today, Treasures for Tomorrow: Overcoming Adversities in Life.*" A perfect title for the story of a courageous woman.[18]

I would like Janet to meet my friend Claire. They have much in common, for they both have incredible, persevering spirits. Claire never felt safe as a child. Her mother was a recurrent source of abuse, betrayal, and violence. Her father divorced her mother and left Claire alone to try to survive and to protect and parent her younger brother.

Claire was motivated to succeed in school so that

she could leave home. She was able to get a scholarship
to college, but halfway through her first year, she had to
drop out because of a blood disorder. At age twenty-one
she was diagnosed with lupus, an autoimmune disease
that attacks normal tissue. Because of her lupus, at age
twenty-three she had to have her spleen and one ovary
removed as well as one tube tied. All this time her mother was in and out of her life.

Claire married Mike, and they adopted two children. Things went well until their three-year-old
developed a tumor and had to have brain surgery.
Then after several years, Claire's past came back to
haunt her. She describes this time as entering a dark
tunnel. She sought help by going to counseling, but
while she was emerging from this tunnel, she became
quite sick. The doctor's diagnosis this time was that
she was pregnant—something that was not supposed to
ever happen.

As if contending with her emotions and morning sickness was not enough to handle, Claire discovered that she had a grapefruit-sized tumor on her
good ovary. Life was nearly unbearable. Here she was
pregnant, fighting lupus, and now facing a precarious
surgery to remove a tumor. Miraculously, both Claire

and her son survived the surgery. Her little boy is now in school.

But this is not the end of my dear friend's story. Recently, she has been diagnosed with primary cirrhosis of the liver. This is a result of her body's turning on itself. She is on additional medication and will eventually have to have a liver transplant.

I was with her the other day and asked about a rash she had around her eye. She proudly told me that the doctor said that the rash was a common one and easily treatable. She was proud because this was one of the few times that she has ever had a "common" disease.

It takes courage to get up every day and live triumphantly with circumstances that will never change. Steadfastness and moral strength are the defining characteristics of women who continue to face adversity with confidence and resolution. These women are uncommonly beautiful.

> *One isn't necessarily born with courage, but one is born with potential. Without courage, we cannot practice any other virtue with consistency. We can't be kind, true, merciful, generous, or honest.*
>
> MAYA ANGELOU

Courage to Be Honest with Ourselves

We have looked at the various facets of courage—standing firm against injustice, seeing it through in the midst of enemy attack, and enduring great personal hardship. But one more aspect of courage needs to be addressed: courage to be honest with ourselves.

There is no one better than Jane Austen to give us a character who comes to see herself as she really is. Elizabeth Bennett of *Pride and Prejudice* is clever, witty, sensitive, and, without realizing it, prone to both pride and prejudice. The account of Elizabeth's finding true love with Mr. Darcy is one of the foremost love stories in literature. These two must overcome the obstacle of class, misunderstanding, and their personal failings of pride and prejudice.

Darcy's wealth and haughty attitude made Elizabeth prejudiced against him from the very beginning, and this colored everything she saw and heard about him in the future. Eventually, in a very direct and fumbling manner, Darcy proposed, and Elizabeth self-righteously refused him. She justified her action by blaming him for making Jane unhappy because he convinced Mr. Bingley that Jane was not interested in him. She also questioned Darcy's dealings with Mr. Wickham—someone she liked and whom she felt Darcy had mistreated.

Elizabeth's journey to self-revelation began with a letter from Darcy, as he attempted to answer her objections. As she read Darcy's honest appraisal of Jane and her relationship to Bingley, and as she began to see Wickham's true character, she was humbled. Austen writes, "She grew absolutely ashamed of herself. Of neither Darcy nor Wickham could she think, without feeling that she had been blind, partial, prejudiced, absurd. 'How despicably I have acted!' she cried. 'I, who have prided myself on my discernment! I, who have valued myself on my abilities! Who have often disdained the generous candour of my sister, and gratified my vanity, in useless or blameless distrust. How humiliating is this discovery! Yet, how just a humiliation! Had I been in love, I could not have been more wretchedly blind. But vanity, not love, has been my folly. . . . Till this moment, I never knew myself.'"[19]

To realize one's own faults takes courage. Elizabeth was finally willing to look at her own heart and admit what she saw.

In her book *Heroines: The Lives of Great Literary Characters and What They Have to Teach Us,* Mary Riso writes, "Lizzy has the courage to realize that when all is said and done, she perhaps does not know everything. She is also not the center of her own life. The willingness to bring perspective and humor to life's troubles communicates a delightful objectivity and freedom from self that requires courage and practice and is worthy of imitation."[20]

It is never too late to be what you might have been.[21]

GEORGE ELIOT

Becoming a Woman of Courage

Maya Angelou believes that courage is the capstone for all the virtues. In reality it takes courage to be passionate enough to take risks, to step out of our comfort zone and seek wisdom, to maintain our integrity in the midst of pretense, to be selfless in a "me first" world, to be gracious to all, to be contented with what is available, and to be honest with ourselves and realistic about the world we live in.

In essence it takes courage to live in today's world. We do travel a rock-strewn road where stress, fear, and trials abound. Sometimes we persevere and nothing seems to change, and it is easy to lose heart. It's important to understand that exercising courage doesn't mean that we always succeed, but it does mean that we are willing to hold our own and to keep moving forward. Anne Morrow Lindbergh wrote, "It takes as much courage to have tried and failed as it does to have tried and succeeded."[22] How true. Susan B. Anthony and Elizabeth Cady Stanton are good examples of courageous women who tried but in their lifetime appeared to have failed.

> *Courage doesn't mean that we always succeed, but it does mean that we are willing to hold our own and to keep moving forward.*

I think that courage is caring enough to risk everything for what is true and good. It is being passionate yet wise in selflessly giving of ourselves when the need arises. It is being honest about ourselves to the point that we can see our imperfections, admit when we are wrong, and be willing to change.

There are no courses in courage, only role models who can inspire and encourage us to follow in their footsteps. And what would these women want to tell us about how to be courageous? I think they would say, "Choose to endure and confront whatever you encounter with integrity, wisdom, passion, and grace. It is in knowing yourself well that you can reach down deep into your soul and find strength to meet each difficulty with dignity and determination. It is deciding that life cannot and will not overwhelm you."

We have Dolley, Gladys, Harriet, Vanessa, Janet, and Claire to challenge and remind us that courage enables us to scale the hardest peaks and to transform every stumbling block into a stepping-stone. It is true that without courage we cannot practice any other virtue with consistency, for courage breathes life into all the other qualities and bestows a beauty that is distinctively uncommon.

> *Courage is not simply one of the virtues but the form of every virtue at the testing point.*[23]
>
> C. S. LEWIS

Questions for Reflection and Discussion

1. How would you define a woman of courage?

2. How does our culture view courage?

3. In your experience, who models or has modeled courage for you?

4. In what ways do other people consider you to be a woman of courage?

5. In what ways would you like to become a woman of courage?

6. What steps can you take to nurture courage in your life?

Uncommon Beauty

True beauty is rare, and seldom
recognized by the one who possesses it.[1]

FRANCINE RIVERS

While sorting through some old papers recently, I came across a slip of yellowed paper entitled "New Year's Resolutions." I had apparently written the list when I was eight years old.

1. Get a boyfriend.
2. Do unto others as you would have them do unto you.
3. Get a figure.
4. Don't say anything mean about other people.

5. Don't eat many sweets as to get a beautiful
   complexion.
6. Do exercises.
7. Good posture.

I smiled as I read these resolutions written in
1947. As I looked back at that time in my life, I realized
that perhaps some values never change. I had already
decided that physical beauty was important: a figure,
nice complexion, and good posture all for the obvious
purpose of getting a boyfriend! Even though I didn't
know the French proverb "Beauty, unaccompanied
by virtue, is a flower without perfume," I did realize
the inherent beauty found in the Golden Rule and in
speaking kindly.

Sixty years later, I can say that I did succeed in
getting a boyfriend—a permanent one—but the other
resolutions are still useful. Eating wisely and exercising consistently are still necessary. I continue to
work on good posture with the help of my daughter's
reminders. But the inner qualities are much more
important to me now, and this book is evidence of
my desire to develop these qualities and to be a sweet
fragrance to all I meet.

We live in deeds, not years; in thoughts, not breaths;
In feelings, not in figures on a dial.
We should count time by heart-throbs. He most lives
Who thinks most, feels the noblest, acts the best.[2]

PHILIP JAMES BAILEY

Uncommon Beauty in the Face of Tragedy

Irene Miller was a young homemaker with a devoted husband, two children, and a normal life in Johnson City, Tennessee. But during the summer of 1950 her son, David Kent, was stricken with bulbar poliomyelitis and was immediately placed in an iron lung. He eventually learned to breathe while being in a wheelchair, but he remained dependent on the respirator every night while he slept.

Three years after polio invaded this young family, the unthinkable happened. In August 1953 Irene's husband, Bud Miller, an insurance salesman, was robbed and murdered. The cash insurance premiums he had collected that day were never recovered, and the crime was never solved.

Irene, who never remarried, undertook the

challenges of single parenting and rearing her daughter, Dolores, and her quadriplegic son. She worked at home as a seamstress so that she could meet her son's needs. With the help of tutors, David graduated from high school, and after learning to type with an electric typewriter, he earned a teaching degree and accepted a position at the county school to teach fourth grade. During all this time, Irene was there for David to drive him to his classes and to assist him with special activities.

For her contribution to his achievement, Irene was honored as Tennessee's "Mother of the Year" in 1971. She certainly deserved this honor, for she approached every situation by seeing the potential, not the limitation. After David died at age thirty-one of heart failure, Irene cared for her aging mother-in-law, then her parents.

Convinced that God had a purpose for her life, Irene made the most of each day. A poem taped to her mirror summarized her outlook: "This is the beginning of a new day. I can waste it or use it for good, but what I do today is important because I am exchanging a day of my life for it. When tomorrow comes, this day will be gone forever, leaving in its place something I have traded for. I want it to be gain and not loss;

success and not failure in order that I shall not forget the price I paid for today."[3]

Irene's life radiated with uncommon beauty. She lived "in deeds, not years; in thoughts, not breaths; in feelings, not in figures on a dial."

> *A virtuous woman is a woman of resolution, who, having espoused good principles, is firm and steady to them, and will not be frightened with winds and clouds from any part of her duty.*[4]

MATTHEW HENRY

Uncommon Beauty Personified

One of my role models for becoming a woman of inner beauty is the description of a virtuous woman found in the last chapter of the Old Testament book of Proverbs. An unknown mother instructs her son, a king, about the essential qualities of a worthy wife. The characteristics that she affirms are universal and apply to all women, regardless of marital status.

Toward the close of the mother's discourse, she warns her son about the deceptiveness of charm and the vanity of beauty. The beauty she emphasizes is the beauty of the spirit. If we look closely we can find the seven qualities of a beautiful woman.

The woman's *passion* is illustrated by her whole-hearted work. She is a diligent yet creative worker. She finds unusual and varied food items for her family. "She finds wool and flax and busily spins it. She is like a merchant's ship, bringing her food from afar. . . . She is energetic and strong, a hard worker."[5]

This woman's *wisdom* enables her to make intelligent business decisions. She also thinks before she speaks, carefully choosing her words. "She goes out to inspect a field and buys it; with her earnings she plants a vineyard. . . . When she speaks, her words are wise."[6]

Her *integrity* is demonstrated by her trustworthiness. Her family has confidence in her. "Her husband can trust her, and she will greatly enrich his life. She brings him good, not harm, all the days of her life. . . . She has no fear of winter for her household, for everyone has warm clothes."[7]

She is *selfless* in serving others. "She extends a helping hand to the poor and opens her arms to the needy."[8]

Her *graciousness* is illustrated by her kindness when speaking and her readiness to be hospitable. "The teaching of kindness is on her tongue. She looks well to the ways of her household, and does not eat the bread of idleness."[9]

I think this woman was very *contented* with her life, for she was strong, honorable, and appreciated. "She is clothed with strength and dignity. . . . Her children stand and bless her. Her husband praises her: 'There are many virtuous and capable women in the world, but you surpass them all!'"[10]

This excellent woman was *courageous*, for she was not anxious about the future. "She laughs without fear of the future."[11] She knew that no matter what happened, she would be able to endure because she could trust God. The foundation of her life was her fear, her reverence, her respect for God.

We know this is true because at the beginning of this passage we are told that this Proverbs 31 woman is "more precious than rubies."[12] What made her life so valuable and special? A verse at the end of the passage gives us the answer: "Charm is deceptive, and beauty does not last; but a woman who fears the Lord will be greatly praised."[13] She was praised for the respect and reverence she gave to God as the creator and sustainer of life. She was commended for honoring God by loving and serving others.

For me, fearing the Lord is acknowledging him as the true God, who alone is worthy of worship. It is believing that God so loved us all that he sent Jesus Christ to reconcile us to himself.[14] It is recognizing that fearing God "is the beginning of wisdom." It is knowing that when I "fear" God, then I am free from all other fears.

> *But the fear of God reigning in the heart is the beauty of the soul;*
> *it recommends those that have it to the favour of God, and is, in his*
> *sight, of great price; it will last for ever, and bid defiance to death*
> *itself, which consumes the beauty of the body, but consummates the*
> *beauty of the soul.*[15]

MATTHEW HENRY

Walking in Uncommon Beauty

When I was a senior in college, I took a course entitled "Byron, Shelley, and Keats." As I studied each of these great authors' writings, Lord Byron's poem "She Walks in Beauty" became one of my favorites. The first few lines give this picture:

> *She walks in beauty, like the night*
> *Of cloudless climes and starry skies,*
> *And all that's best of dark and bright*
> *Meet in her aspect and her eyes....*

The final lines round out the image:

And on that cheek and o'er that brow
So soft, so calm yet eloquent,
The smiles that win, the tints that glow
But tell of days in goodness spent,
A mind at peace with all below,
A heart whose love is innocent.[16]

What a charming tribute to a lovely lady. I appreciate the image of this woman walking in beauty. Byron discerns that beauty is a way of life; it is a lifestyle. Wherever this woman was and whatever she did, she walked in beauty. Her soft, calm spirit, her smile, her goodness, a mind at peace, and a heart of innocent love are the measure of her attractiveness. All seven qualities are there: her smiles and tints that glow speak of her passion, her days in goodness spent speak of her wisdom, integrity, selflessness, and graciousness. The mind at peace is indicative of her contentment, and her courage is exemplified by her commitment to walk in beauty and love.

Byron portrays a woman of multiple qualities that together produce a true and uncommon beauty. As we

have observed in the lives of the women we have studied, the qualities spill over into each other—supporting,
sharpening, and shaping the soul so that it is whole and
complete and beautiful.

> *The seven qualities spill over into*
> *each other—supporting, sharpening,*
> *and shaping the soul so that it is whole*
> *and complete and beautiful.*

Christa McAuliffe was passionate, but she was also
selfless, contented, and courageous. Florence Nightingale was not only wise but also passionate, selfless,
and courageous. Abigail was a woman of integrity, but
she was wise, selfless, gracious, and courageous as well.
Selflessness was the hallmark of Amy Carmichael's life,
but she was also passionate, wise, committed to doing
what was right, contented, and very courageous. Dolley
Madison was not only gracious but also courageous,
contented, passionate, selfless, and wise. Ruth exemplified contentment, but she was also selfless, wise,
gracious, a woman of integrity, and courageous.

I am sure that Irene never considered herself

beautiful, but beautiful she was, for she personified all seven qualities. Her passion was to live each day to its fullest. Her wisdom and integrity were shown by her desire to use each day for good. She was selfless and gracious in giving her life for her family. She chose to accept what could not be changed and to live a productive life in spite of her circumstances. Her courage in the face of adversity was the foundation of every virtue at the testing point.

Uncommon beauty is sown and cultivated in the soul. It is watered by passion and wisdom. It puts down deep roots by practicing integrity. It flourishes by being selfless and gracious to others. It grows strong by staying firmly planted in its circumstances and courageously enduring the clouds and wind.

> *Uncommon beauty is sown and cultivated in the soul.*

So the choice is ours. We can sow the seed of each of these qualities in our soul so that we can bloom with the lovely flower of uncommon beauty.

The soul's *soil* that allows these qualities to blossom is love. Love undergirds each of the seven qualities. Love sustains passion. Love inspires wisdom. Love strengthens integrity. Love empowers selfless-ness. Love encourages graciousness. Love nourishes contentment. Love energizes courage. Without the pervasive power of love propelling us to desire these qualities, we would be incomplete.

Love enriches each quality and helps to provide that "certain something" and "air" that produces uncommon beauty. And it is this extraordinary, price-less beauty that we really want for our lives. All of the spa treatments in the world cannot keep us young or make us truly beautiful. As a quotation at the beginning of this book reminded us, "But if you are beautiful at sixty, it will be your soul's own doing."[17]

We know it can be done because we have the exam-ple of ordinary women who have lived uncommonly beautiful lives. As I think of these women, I doubt that most of them would have considered themselves beautiful. I agree with Francine Rivers's observation, "True beauty is rare, and seldom recognized by the one who possesses it." Perhaps this truth expresses the heart of uncommonly beautiful women. They are more concerned about living passionately and wisely, they think of others more than themselves, they thrive in their circumstances, and they value freedom and justice over their own desires. To be known as beautiful would surprise them.

My desire for this book is that you will have a clear picture of the significance and blessing of inner beauty. And my desire for you, dear reader, is that you will begin from this day forward to walk in beauty, grow inwardly more lovely, and become an uncommonly beautiful woman.

> *Remember that when you leave this earth, you can take with you nothing that you have received—only what you have given: a full heart enriched by honest service, love, sacrifice and courage.*[18]

ST. FRANCIS OF ASSISI

Questions for Reflection and Discussion

1. What have you learned about beauty through reading the chapters in this book?

2. What have you learned about your own inner beauty?

3. What would you consider to be the foundation of beauty in your life?

4. What people and experiences in your life help to nurture beauty in you?

5. In what ways would you like to grow more uncommonly beautiful?

Optional Bible Study for the Seven Qualities

In order to have a biblical context about the qualities of uncommon beauty, use the following Bible verses along with the questions at the end of each chapter to facilitate personal study and group discussion. As you look at each passage, write down what the verse says to you about the quality.

A Certain Something

When we desire to rise above the clamor of the world and seek the beauty of the Lord, we will obtain that "certain something" that will last.

> 1 Samuel 16:7
> Romans 12:2
> Colossians 2:8-10
> 1 Peter 3:3-4

Passion

Passion finds its ultimate reward when it is directed toward God and his Kingdom.

> Psalm 119:111-112
> Matthew 6:33
> 2 Corinthians 5:9
> Colossians 3:23

Wisdom

The foundation of true wisdom is the desire to know and acknowledge God in our lives.

> Proverbs 2:1-11
> Proverbs 9:10
> Colossians 2:2-3
> James 3:17

Integrity

There is no substitute for integrity in living a life that pleases God.

> Proverbs 10:9
> Proverbs 11:3
> Acts 24:15-16
> 1 Peter 2:15-17

Selflessness

God lovingly asks us to trust him, surrender control of our lives, and live selflessly.

> Luke 9:23-25
> Romans 14:7-8
> Galatians 2:20
> Ephesians 4:21-24

Graciousness

When we are gracious, we reflect the heart of God.

> Psalm 86:5
> Ephesians 1:7-8
> Ephesians 2:4-10
> Ephesians 4:31-32

Contentment

Whatever our "lot" or circumstance, contentment enables us to sing "It is well with my soul."

> Psalm 73:25-26
> Philippians 3:5-9
> Philippians 4:10-13
> Hebrews 13:5-6

Courage

Courage is confidently moving forward, strengthened by the power of God.

> Isaiah 41:10
> 2 Corinthians 12:7-10
> Philippians 4:13
> Colossians 1:11-12

Uncommon Beauty

Spiritual beauty blesses its bearer and all whom she meets.

> 1 Corinthians 13:4-7
> 1 Corinthians 16:13-14
> Ephesians 3:14-21
> 1 Timothy 2:9-10

✿ Notes

A Certain Something

1. Marie Stoops, in *She Said, She Said: Strong Words from Strong-Minded Women,* comp. and ed. Gloria Adler (New York: Avon Books, 1995), 17.
2. Jane Austen, *Pride and Prejudice* (London: Collins, 1952), 46.
3. Ruth Bell Graham, *Footprints of a Pilgrim* (Nashville: Word, 2001), 27.
4. William Shakespeare, *The Sonnets* (New York: Gramercy Books, 1991), Sonnet LIV, 52.
5. French Proverb, in *The New Book of Christian Quotations,* comp. Tony Castle (New York: Crossroad, 1989), 19.
6. Graham, *Footprints of a Pilgrim,* 27.
7. 1 Samuel 16:7.
8. Cecil Beaton, in *Bartlett's Book of Anecdotes,* eds. Clifton Fadiman and Andre Bernard (New York: Little, Brown, and Company, 1985), 191.
9. Herbert Spencer, in *The New Book of Christian Quotations,* comp. Tony Castle (New York: Crossroad, 1989), 19.
10. Ralph Waldo Emerson, "Art," *Essays: First Series*; see also www .emersoncentral.com/art.htm.

Chapter 1: Passion

1. Louisa May Alcott, in *The Last Word: A Treasury of Women's Quotes,* comp. Carolyn Warner (Englewood Cliffs, N.J.: Prentice Hall, 1992), 303.

2. Edna St. Vincent Millay, "Renascence," in *The Last Word,* comp. Carolyn Warner (Englewood Cliffs, N.J.: Prentice Hall, 1992), 306.

3. "Christa McAuliffe: A Biography," Christa McAuliffe Planetarium; see www.starhop.com/cm_bio.htm.

4. Grace Corrigan, *A Journal for Christa: Christa McAuliffe, Teacher in Space* (Lincoln, Neb.: University of Nebraska Press, 1993), xii.

5. Joan Baez, in *The Last Word,* comp. Carolyn Warner (Englewood Cliffs, N.J.: Prentice Hall, 1992), 59.

6. Deborah G. Felder, *The 100 Greatest Women of All Time* (Oxford, England: Past Times, 1998), 51–53.

7. Ibid., 96–97.

8. Sophocles, *Antigone,* trans. Richard Emil Braun (New York: Oxford University Press, 1973), I. 571–73.

9. Anais Nin, in *She Said, She Said: Strong Words from Strong-Minded Women,* comp. and ed. Gloria Adler (New York: Avon Books, 1995), 40.

10. Read Priscilla's story in Acts 18.

11. Emily Dickinson, "XIV. Aspiration," in *The Last Word,* comp. Carolyn Warner (Englewood Cliffs, N.J.: Prentice Hall, 1992), 53.

12. Herbert Lockyer, *All the Women of the Bible* (Grand Rapids: Zondervan, 1996), 74.

13. Sara Blakely, in *The Trident* 115, no. 3 (Spring 2006): 41.

14. Hunter S. Thompson, see www.quotationsandsayings.com.

Chapter 2: Wisdom

1. Sandra Carey, in *She Said, She Said: Strong Words from Strong-Minded Women,* comp. and ed. Gloria Adler (New York: Avon Books, 1995), 154.

2. Proverbs 11:22.

3. Proverbs 8:11.

4. William Richmond, *The Richmond Papers,* in Deborah G. Felder, *The 100 Greatest Women of All Time* (Oxford, England: Past Times, 1998), 76.

5. Quoted from *Selections from The Arabian Nights,* trans. Sir Richard Francis Burton (Garden City, N.Y.: International Collectors Library, nd), 12.

6. Ibid., 13.

7. Ibid., 20–1.

8. Ibid., 43.

9. Cate Blanchett, in "Cate Shines," *Harper's Bazaar* (August 2005), 146, 150.

10. To read the entire story of the queen, see 1 Kings 10:1-13 and 2 Chronicles 9:1-12.

11. Proverbs 16:16.

12. 1 Kings 10:2-5.

13. Ben Sira, in *Never Scratch a Tiger with a Short Stick* (Colorado Springs: NavPress, 2003), 200.

14. Read Rebekah's story in Genesis 27:1-40.

15. Genesis 27:13.

16. Proverbs 14:1.

17. Proverbs 13:16.

18. Marilyn vos Savant, in Quotations Page, http://www.quotationspage. com/quote/3164.html. Marilyn vos Savant, whose weekly column appears in *Parade Magazine,* is reported to have the highest IQ ever recorded.

19. Antonio de Guevara, in *Dictionary of Quotations*, comp. Bergen Evans (New York: Avenel Books, 1978), 756.

20. John Phillips, *Exploring Proverbs*, vol. 1 (Grand Rapids: Kregel, 1995), 44.

21. Proverbs 13:20, THE MESSAGE.

22. Proverbs 8:11, THE MESSAGE.

23. Proverbs 4:6-9, THE MESSAGE.

Chapter 3: Integrity

1. Jacqueline Bisset, *Los Angeles Times,* May 16, 1974.

2. Rosa Parks, see http://en.wikipedia.org/wiki/Rosa_Parks.

3. Ibid.

4. Deborah G. Felder, *The 100 Greatest Women of All Time* (Oxford, England: Past Times, 1998), 63.

5. William Shakespeare, *Hamlet, Prince of Denmark* (New York: Appleton-Century-Crofts, Inc., 1946), act I, scene III, lines 85–87.

6. Charlotte Brontë, *Jane Eyre* (New York: Random House, 1943), 259.

7. Ibid.

8. Ibid., 309.

9. Janis Joplin, in *The Last Word: A Treasury of Women's Quotes,* comp. Carolyn Warner (Englewood Cliffs, N.J.: Prentice Hall, 1992), 54.

10. To read the entire story of Abigail, see 1 Samuel 25:1-44.

11. 1 Samuel 25:3, NLT(96).

12. 1 Samuel 25:24-25.

13. Proverbs 10:9, NLT(96).

14. Read the story in Genesis 39.

15. Genesis 39:14-18, NLT(96).

16. Harper Lee, *The Last Word,* comp. Carolyn Warner (Englewood Cliffs, N.J.: Prentice Hall, 1992), 54.

17. Anne Morrow Lindbergh, in *The American Experience*; see http://www.pbs.org/wgbh/amex/lindbergh/sfeature/anne.html.

18. Joan Didion, *The Last Word,* comp. Carolyn Warner (Englewood Cliffs, N.J.: Prentice Hall, 1992), 251.

Chapter 4: Selflessness

1. Ethel Percy Andrus, *The Last Word: A Treasury of Women's Quotes,* comp. Carolyn Warner (Englewood Cliffs, N.J.: Prentice Hall, 1992), 139.

2. Helen Kooiman Hosier, *100 Christian Women Who Changed the Twentieth Century* (Grand Rapids: Revel, 2000), 251.

3. Psalm 34:22, KJV.

4. Philippians 2:7, KJV.

5. Hosier, *100 Christian Women Who Changed the Twentieth Century,* 249.

6. Jewish Women's Archives. "JWA: Henrietta Szold: An Icon"; see http://www.jwa.org/exhibits/wov/szold/icon.html.

7. Amy Carmichael, in *Worth Repeating,* comp. Bob Kelly (Grand Rapids: Kregel, 2003), 137.

8. O. Henry, "The Gift of the Magi," *The Pocket Book of O. Henry Stories*, ed. Harry Hansen (New York: Washington Square Press, 1962), 2.

9. Ibid., 5.

10. Ibid., 6.

11. *Apples of Gold*, comp. Jo Petty (Norwalk, Conn.: C. R. Gibson Co., 1962), 57.

12. Helen Keller, in *The 100 Greatest Women of All Time* (Oxford, England: Past Times, 1998), 68.

13. Helen Keller, in Deborah G. Felder, *The New Book of Christian Quotations*, comp. Tony Castle (New York: Crossroad, 1989), 247.

14. Read Esther's exciting story in the Old Testament book of Esther.

15. Esther 4:11, NLT(96).

16. Esther 4:16, NLT(96).

17. Carolyn Warner, *The Last Word,* comp. Carolyn Warner (Englewood Cliffs, N.J.: Prentice Hall, 1992), 54.

18. Read more about Narcissus at http://en.wikipedia.org/wiki/Narcissus_(mythology).

19. Kate Halverson, in *She Said, She Said: Strong Words from Strong-Minded Women,* comp. and ed. Gloria Adler (New York: Avon Books, 1995), 147.

20. Luke 1:38, THE MESSAGE.

21. Story told by Donna Savage, a pastor's wife, freelance writer, and speaker living in Nevada. Contact her at donnasavagelv@cox.net.

22. Story told by Larisee Lynn Stevens, a published author and experienced speaker. Learn more about her at her web site: http://www.spokenfitly.com.

23. Jane Austen, *Pride and Prejudice* (New York: Penguin Books, 1985), 377.

24. Alice R. Pratt, in *Quotable Quotations,* comp. Lloyd Cory (Wheaton, Ill.: Victor, 1985), 155.

Chapter 5: Graciousness

1. Mary Ann Kelty, *The Last Word: A Treasury of Women's Quotes,* comp. Carolyn Warner (Englewood Cliffs, N.J.: Prentice Hall, 1992), 54.

2. Hada Bejar, see http://www.quoteland.com/topic.asp?CATEGORY_ID=64.

3. All quotations in the Bobbi Olson story are from *Tucson Citizen,* January 5, 2001, 4A.

4. This headline appeared in *Tucson Citizen,* January 2, 2001, 7A.

5. Michel Quoist, in *Quotes for the Journey, Wisdom for the Way,* comp. Gordon S. Jackson (Colorado Springs: NavPress, 2000), 106.

6. See http://www.who2.com/dolleymadison.html.

7. The White House Historical Association, The First Ladies: Dolley Madison, at http://www.whitehousehistory.org/05/subs/05_b02.html; The White House, Past First Ladies, Dolley Payne Todd Madison, at http://www.whitehouse.gov/history/firstladies/dm4.html.

8. John Milton, *Paradise Lost* (New York: W. W. Norton, 1993), bk. VIII, lines 488–89.

9. Read the story of Lydia in Acts 16:13-40.

10. Proverbs 11:17, NLT(96).

11. Flannery O'Connor, in *Quotes for the Journey,* 74.

12. Read Peninnah's story in 1 Samuel 1:1-28.

13. 1 Samuel 1:6-7.

14. Charlotte Brontë, *Jane Eyre* (New York: Barnes and Noble Books, 2003), 89.

15. William Shakespeare, *The Tragedy of King Lear* (New York: Washington Square Press, 1993), act I, scene I, line 85.

16. Ibid., act IV, scene VII, lines 81–85.

17. Mark Twain, in *Quotes for the Journey,* 59.

18. Paula Rinehart, *Strong Women, Soft Hearts* (Nashville: Word, 2001), 112.

19. Joan Lunden, in *Treasury of Wit & Wisdom,* comp. Jeff Bredenberg (Pleasantville, N.Y.: Reader's Digest Association, 2006), 70.

20. A survivor of sexual abuse, quoted in Diane Mandt Langberg, *On the Threshold of Hope* (Wheaton, Ill.: Tyndale, 1999), 174.

21. William Shakespeare, *The Merchant of Venice,* in *The Oxford Shakespeare,* ed.

W. J. Craig (London: University Press, 1914) act IV, scene I, lines
80–84.

Chapter 6: Contentment

1. Charles Dickens, *Barnaby Rudge* (London: Waverley Book Co., n.d.), 365.
2. Annie Dillard, in *Treasury of Wit and Wisdom,* comp. Jeff Bredenberg
   (Pleasantville, N.Y.: Reader's Digest Association, 2006), 115.
3. Martha Washington, in *The Last Word: A Treasury of Women's Quotes,* comp.
   Carolyn Warner (Englewood Cliffs, N.J.: Prentice Hall, 1992), 149.
4. Philippians 4:11.
5. Natalie Pompilio, "Heroes of the Hurricane," *Reader's Digest* (November
   2005): 99–100.
6. Ellen Glasgow, in *The Last Word,* comp. Carolyn Warner (Englewood
   Cliffs, N.J.: Prentice Hall, 1992), 35.
7. Laura Ingalls Wilder, *Little House on the Prairie* (New York: Harper
   Trophy, 1971), 131.
8. Epictetus, in *Quotable Quotations,* comp. Lloyd Cory (Wheaton, Ill.:
   Victor, 1985), 82.
9. Jane Austen, *Pride and Prejudice* (New York: Penguin Books, 1985), 175.
10. Ibid., 359.
11. Gerald R. Payne, in *Megiddo Message* 86, no. 8 (Sept/October 1999): 9.
12. To read the entire story of Ruth, read the four chapters of the book
    of Ruth.
13. Ruth 1:16.
14. Ruth 3:10–11, NASB.
15. Irving Fineman, quoted in Edith Deen, *All of the Women of the Bible* (New
    York: Harper, 1955), 82.
16. For these statistics and others, see the report based on "Who Lives in
    the Global Village?" at http://www.familycare.org/news.
17. James 4:14, THE MESSAGE. In the chapter about contentment I
    mentioned a Scripture passage that states we are nothing but wisps of
    fog catching a brief bit of sun before disappearing (James 4:14). This

thought can be somewhat disheartening until we understand that
believing in Christ gives us eternal life with him forever. But while
we are wisps of fog here on earth, we can experience the abundant life
that only God can give and be graced with his presence which makes all
those who truly love and reverence him uncommonly beautiful.

18. Even though we are wisps of fog here on earth, the good news is that
this life is not all there is. God promises eternal life to all who believe
in him (see John 3:16).

19. Diana Krall, quoting Joni Mitchell, "Quotable Quotes," *Reader's Digest*
(May 2006): 73.

Chapter 7: Courage

1. Gail Brook Burket, in *The Last Word: A Treasury of Women's Quotes,* comp.
Carolyn Warner (Englewood Cliffs, N.J.: Prentice Hall, 1992), 76.

2. William J. Bennett, *The Book of Virtues* (New York: Simon & Schuster,
1993), 481–83.

3. Ambrose Redmoon, in *Worth Repeating,* comp. Bob Kelly (Grand
Rapids: Kregel, 2003), 68.

4. Gregory Feifer, "For Chechen Villagers, Conflict Doesn't End,"
Morning Edition, National Public Radio, August 2, 2006.

5. William J. Bennett, *The Moral Compass* (New York: Simon & Schuster,
1995), 301–303.

6. Deborah G. Felder, *The 100 Greatest Women of All Time* (Oxford, England:
Past Times, 1998), 31–33.

7. Kerry Kennedy interview with Juliana Dogbadzi, "Speak to Power," at
http://www.washingtonpost.com/wp-srv/photo/onassignment/truth/
st/09.htm.

8. Kerry Kennedy interview with Juliana Dogbadzi, "Speak to Power,"
at http://www.speaktruth.org/defend/profiles/profile_02.asp.

9. Eleanor Roosevelt, in *She Said, She Said: Strong Words from Strong-Minded
Women,* ed. Gloria Adler (New York: Avon Books, 1995), 136.

10. "Please note that although *The Inn of the Sixth Happiness* is a well-produced,

heartwarming movie . . . it was a thorn in the side of Gladys Aylward. She was deeply embarrassed by the movie because it was so full of inaccuracies. . . . Gladys, the most chaste of women, was horrified to learn the movie had portrayed her in 'love scenes.' She suffered greatly over what she considered her soiled reputation." Sam Wellman's biography site at http://www.heroesofhistory.com/page46.html.

11. Sam Wellman, *Gladys Aylward* (Uhrichsville, Ohio: Barbour, 1998).

12. To read the full story of Jehosheba, see 2 Chronicles 21:10–23:11.

13. "The Mom," *Reader's Digest* (January 2006): 29–30.

14. Harper Lee, *To Kill a Mockingbird* (New York: Harper & Row, 1960), 121.

15. Deborah G. Felder, *The 100 Greatest Women of All Time*, (Oxford, England: Past Times, 1998) 28–30.

16. William J. Bennett, *The Book of Virtues* (New York: Simon & Schuster, 1993), 485–88.

17. Catherine Boyle, author of *Hungry Souls: What the Bible Says about Eating Disorder*, lives in the Richmond, Virginia, area with her husband, Barney, and two children. Contact Catherine at www.catherineboyle.com.

18. Janet Perez Eckles, a national inspirational speaker and writer for regional and national Christian magazines, lives in Orlando, Florida, and can be contacted at www.janeckles.com.

19. Jane Austen, *Pride and Prejudice* (New York: Penguin Books, 1985), 236.

20. Mary Riso, *Heroines: The Lives of Great Literary Characters and What They Have to Teach Us* (Grand Rapids: Baker, 2003), 90.

21. George Eliot, in *Worth Repeating*, 265.

22. Anne Morrow Lindbergh, in *Worth Repeating*, 67.

23. C. S. Lewis, in *Never Scratch a Tiger with a Short Stick* (Colorado Springs: NavPress, 2003), 46.

Uncommon Beauty

1. Francine Rivers, *A Voice in the Wind* (Wheaton, Ill.: Tyndale, 1993), 66.

2. Philip James Bailey, *Festus*, scene v.; see http://www.literatureclassics.com/browselitquotes.asp?subcategory=AC&author=Bailey.

3. This story was sent to me by e-mail from Dianne Barker, coauthor of *Twice Pardoned* (with Harold Morris) and *Living Proof* (with Clebe McClary). Contact Dianne at diannebarker@earthlink.net.

4. Matthew Henry, *Matthew Henry's Commentary in One Volume,* ed. Leslie F. Church (Grand Rapids: Zondervan, 1961), 789.

5. Proverbs 31:13-14, 17.

6. Proverbs 31:16, 26.

7. Proverbs 31:11-12, 21.

8. Proverbs 31:20.

9. Proverbs 31:26-27, NASB.

10. Proverbs 31:25, 28-29.

11. Proverbs 31:25.

12. Proverbs 31:10.

13. Proverbs 31:30.

14. When I was twelve years old, I was asked if I believed that Jesus Christ is the Son of God and that he died on the cross for my sins. My answer was yes. I believed the Bible's promise: "For God so loved the world that he gave his only Son, so that everyone who believes in him will not perish but have eternal life" (John 3:16). My simple, heartfelt yes enabled me to be born again. Since that time, I have experienced God's love, forgiveness, and grace in my life, and it has made all the difference. It is because I love and reverence him that I want to be a woman of uncommon beauty.

15. Matthew Henry, *Matthew Henry's Commentary in One Volume,* 976–77.

16. Lord George Gordon Byron, in *Treasury of Great Poems,* comp. Louis Untermeyer (New York: Galahad Books, 1993), 700–701.

17. Marie Stoops, in *She Said, She Said,* comp. and ed. Gloria Adler (New York: Avon Books, 1995), 17.

18. St. Francis of Assisi, in *Quotes for the Journey, Wisdom for the Way,* comp. Gordon S. Jackson (Colorado Springs: NavPress, 2000), 162.

❊ *Acknowledgments*

This book is special to me because it has given me the opportunity to acknowledge women who understood that true beauty does not live in the physical realm but abides deep within a woman's soul and continues to leave a sweet aroma long after the physical has faded away. I am indebted to the women who willingly shared their lives with me and who have taught me the worth of uncommon beauty.

A heartfelt thank you to my family and friends for beautifying my life and for letting me share some of their stories. To my dear Elderberries: thanks for your love and support as you prayed me through another book.

A special thanks to Gail, Huntley, Karen, Trish, and Barb for their interest and excellent suggestions. I am also grateful for the number of authors who were interested in contributing stories of uncommon beauty.

I am grateful to Lynn Vanderzalm, my dear friend and editor, whose special "polish" makes my writing as beautiful as it can be.

Thanks to Katherine Helmers for launching me on this project and for being there for me.

Without the support and encouragement from Tyndale House Publishers, this book could not become a reality. Thank you.

I so appreciate my daughter Shelly for taking the time to read the manuscript and offer her good insights. I also thank my daughter Melinda for her interest and suggestions.

And how could I continue to grow old without my husband, Jack, who continues to make me feel beautiful?

And it is with much gratitude that I thank the Lord for choosing to beautify my life with His presence.

𝒶 *About the Author*

Cynthia Heald uses her speaking engagements, Bible studies,
and books to encourage women
around he world to deepen
their relationship with God. In
addition to herpopular Becoming a Woman Of . . . Bible study
series, which includes the best-selling *Becoming a Woman of
Excellence* and *Becoming a Woman of reedom,* Cynthia has also
written *Abiding in Christ: Becoming a Woman Who Walks with God,*
a Gold Medallion—winning devotional. Her husband,
Jack, joined her in writing two Bible studies about
marriage: *Loving Your Wife* and *Walking Together.* Cynthia's

other nonfiction books include *Maybe God Is Right after All,*
A Woman's Journey to the Heart of God, and *When the Father Holds*
You Close.

When Cynthia is not writing or speaking, she loves
to spend time with Jack and their four children and
eight grandchildren. She is an avid reader, especially of
the classics. Cynthia enjoys taking bubble baths, having
tea parties, and eating out.

Cynthia and Jack are full-time Navigator staff
members in Tucson, Arizona.